WINDOWS® 98

— VISUAL SOLUTIONS —

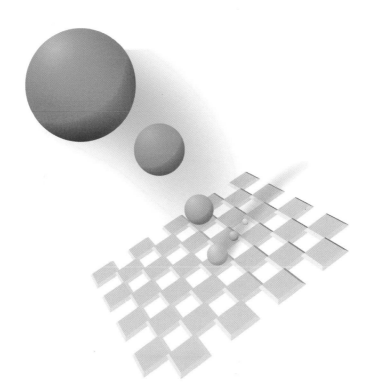

by: maranGraphics' Development Group

Corporate Sales

Contact maranGraphics
Phone: (905) 890-3300
      (800) 469-6616
Fax: (905) 890-9434

Canadian Trade Sales

Contact Prentice Hall Canada
Phone: (416) 293-3621
      (800) 567-3800
Fax: (416) 299-2529

Windows® 98 Visual Solutions

Canadian Cataloguing in Publication Data

Maran, Ruth, 1970-
   Windows 98 : visual solutions

(Visual 3-D series)
Written by Ruth Maran.
Includes index.
ISBN 1-896283-38-1

1. Microsoft Windows (Computerfile).
2. Operating systems (Computers).
I. MaranGraphics Inc. II. Title. III. Series.

QA76.76.W56M3864 1998   005.4'3769   C98-930773-5

Trademark Acknowledgments

maranGraphics Inc. has attempted to include trademark information for products, services and companies referred to in this guide. Although maranGraphics Inc. has made reasonable efforts in gathering this information, it cannot guarantee its accuracy.

All other brand names and product names used in this book are trademarks, registered trademarks, or trade names of their respective holders. maranGraphics Inc. is not associated with any product or vendor mentioned in this book.

FOR PURPOSES OF ILLUSTRATING THE CONCEPTS AND TECHNIQUES DESCRIBED IN THIS BOOK, THE AUTHOR HAS CREATED VARIOUS NAMES, COMPANY NAMES, MAILING ADDRESSES, E-MAIL ADDRESSES AND PHONE NUMBERS, ALL OF WHICH ARE FICTITIOUS. ANY RESEMBLANCE OF THESE FICTITIOUS NAMES, COMPANY NAMES, MAILING ADDRESSES, E-MAIL ADDRESSES AND PHONE NUMBERS TO ANY ACTUAL PERSON, COMPANY AND/OR ORGANIZATION IS UNINTENTIONAL AND PURELY COINCIDENTAL.

Permissions

CNN SI
© 1998 Cable News Network, Inc. All Rights Reserved. Used by permission of CNNSI.
Microsoft
Screen shots reprinted by permission from Microsoft Corporation.
MSNBC Weather Map
© MSNBC on the Internet, 1998.
NHL Hockey 95
Screen Shots from NHL ® 95 © 1994 Electronic Arts Inc. All rights reserved. NHL is a trademark of the National Hockey League and is used under license by Electronic Arts.
Smithsonian
Copyright 1995 by Smithsonian Institution.
Spiegel, Inc.
© Spiegel, Inc. Used by permission.
Sportsline USA
Copyright © 1996 Sportsline USA, Inc. http://www.sportsline.com. All Rights Reserved.
USA Today
Copyright 1996 USA Today Online.
YAHOO!
Text and artwork copyright © 1996 by YAHOO!, INC. All rights reserved. YAHOO! and the YAHOO! logo are trademarks of YAHOO!, INC.

The following companies have also given us permission to use their screen shots:
Discovery Channel Online
Florida Legislature On-Line Sunshine
FlowerStop
JCPenney
Minolta
People Daily Online
Sunkist
Travel Source

© 1998 maranGraphics, Inc.
The 3-D illustrations are the copyright of maranGraphics, Inc.

WINDOWS® 98

— VISUAL SOLUTIONS —

VISUAL SERIES 3D

maranGraphics™

Every maranGraphics book represents
the extraordinary vision and commitment of a unique family:
the Maran family of Toronto, Canada.

Back Row (from left to right): *Sherry Maran, Rob Maran, Richard Maran, Maxine Maran, Jill Maran.*

Front Row (from left to right): *Judy Maran, Ruth Maran.*

Richard Maran is the company founder and its inspirational leader. He developed maranGraphics' proprietary communication technology called "visual grammar." This book is built on that technology—empowering readers with the easiest and quickest way to learn about computers.

Ruth Maran is the Author and Architect—a role Richard established that now bears Ruth's distinctive touch. She creates the words and visual structure that are the basis for the books.

Judy Maran is the Project Coordinator. She works with Ruth, Richard and the highly talented maranGraphics illustrators, designers and editors to transform Ruth's material into its final form.

Rob Maran is the Technical and Production Specialist. He makes sure the state-of-the-art technology used to create these books always performs as it should.

Sherry Maran manages the Reception, Order Desk and any number of areas that require immediate attention and a helping hand.

Jill Maran is a jack-of-all-trades who works in the Accounting and Human Resources department.

Maxine Maran is the Business Manager and family sage. She maintains order in the business and family—and keeps everything running smoothly.

CREDITS

Author & Architect:
Ruth Maran

Copy Development:
Wanda Lawrie

Project Coordinator:
Judy Maran

Editing & Screen Captures:
Roxanne Van Damme
Raquel Scott
Jason M. Brown
Janice Boyer
Cathy Benn
Michelle Kirchner
Brad Hilderley
Marcus McKinney

Layout Designer & Illustrator:
Jamie Bell

Illustrators:
Russ Marini
Treena Lees
Peter Grecco
Ben Lee

Screen Artist:
Jeff Jones

Indexer:
Kelleigh Wing

Post Production:
Robert Maran

ACKNOWLEDGMENTS

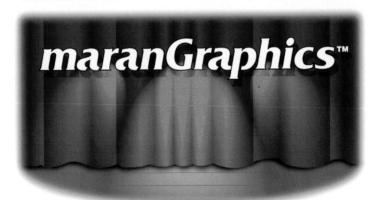

Thanks to the dedicated staff of maranGraphics, including
Jamie Bell, Cathy Benn, Janice Boyer, Jason M. Brown,
Francisco Ferreira, Peter Grecco, Jeff Jones, Michelle Kirchner,
Wanda Lawrie, Treena Lees, Michael W. MacDonald, Jill Maran,
Judy Maran, Maxine Maran, Robert Maran, Sherry Maran,
Russ Marini, Raquel Scott, Susanne Secko, Roxanne Van Damme,
Paul Whitehead and Kelleigh Wing.

Finally, to Richard Maran who originated the easy-to-use
graphic format of this guide. Thank you for your inspiration
and guidance.

TABLE OF CONTENTS

Chapter 1

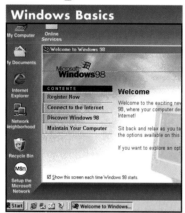

Chapter 2

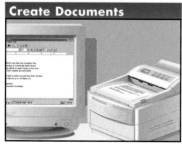

Chapter 3

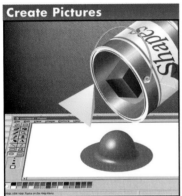

Create Pictures

Chapter 4

View Files

Chapter 5

Work with Files

TABLE OF CONTENTS

Chapter 6

Customize Windows

Chapter 7

Have Fun with Windows

Chapter 8

Optimize Your Computer

Chapter 9

Work on a Network

TABLE OF CONTENTS

Chapter 10

Browse the Web

Chapter 11

Exchange Electronic Mail

Chapter 12

Using Newsgroups

Chapter 13

Create Web Pages

Chapter 14

Work with Channels

Times New Roman (Western)
10
Internet
Explorer
Network
Neighborhood
For Help, press F1
NUM
Start
Document - WordPad
Document - WordPad
File Edit View Insert Format
Times New Roman (Western)

CHAPTER 1

Windows Basics

This chapter will teach you the basic skills you will need to work in Windows 98.

INTRODUCTION TO WINDOWS 98

Microsoft® Windows® 98 is a program that controls the overall activity of your computer.

Windows ensures that all parts of your computer work together smoothly and efficiently.

Work with Files

Windows provides ways to organize and manage the files stored on your computer. You can open, sort, rename, move, print, find and delete files. Windows also allows you to work with files stored on other computers on a network.

Write Letters and Draw Pictures

Windows includes a word processing program, called WordPad, that you can use to write letters. Windows also includes a drawing program, called Paint, that you can use to draw pictures.

Customize Windows

You can customize Windows in many ways. You can add a colorful design to your screen, change the way your mouse works and change the amount of information that fits on the screen.

Have Fun with Windows

You can have fun with Windows. You can play games, play music CDs and assign sounds to program events.

Optimize Your Computer

Windows provides tools to help you optimize your computer. You can check your hard disk for errors, remove unnecessary files and defragment your hard disk to improve its performance.

Exchange E-Mail and Join Newsgroups

Windows allows you to exchange electronic mail with people around the world. You can also join newsgroups which allow people with common interests to communicate with each other.

Browse the Web

Windows lets you browse through the information on the World Wide Web and create your own Web pages. Windows also allows you to work with channels. Channels are specially designed Web sites Windows can automatically deliver to your computer.

PARTS OF THE WINDOWS 98 SCREEN

The Windows 98 screen displays various items. The items that appear depend on how your computer is set up.

My Computer

Lets you view all the folders and files stored on your computer.

My Documents

Provides a convenient place to store your documents.

Network Neighborhood

Lets you view all the folders and files available on your network.

Recycle Bin

Stores deleted files and allows you to recover them later.

Quick Launch Toolbar

Gives you quick access to commonly used features, including Internet Explorer, Outlook Express, the desktop and channels.

Title Bar

Displays the name of an open window.

Window

A rectangle on your screen that displays information.

Desktop

The background area of your screen.

Start Button

Gives you quick access to programs, files and Windows Help.

Taskbar

Displays a button for each open window on your screen. You can use these buttons to switch between open windows.

Channel Bar

Displays specially designed Web sites you can have windows automatically deliver to your computer.

A mouse is a handheld device that lets you select and move items on your screen.

When you move the mouse on your desk, the mouse pointer on your screen moves in the same direction. The mouse pointer assumes different shapes, such as ⬉ or I, depending on its location on your screen and the task you are performing.

Resting your hand on the mouse, use your thumb and two rightmost fingers to move the mouse on your desk. Use your two remaining fingers to press the mouse buttons.

MOUSE ACTIONS

Click

Press and release the left mouse button.

Double-click

Quickly press and release the left mouse button twice.

Right-click

Press and release the right mouse button.

Drag

Position the mouse pointer over an object on your screen and then press and hold down the left mouse button. Still holding down the button, move the mouse to where you want to place the object and then release the button.

START WINDOWS

Windows provides an easy, graphical way for you to use your computer. Windows starts when you turn on your computer.

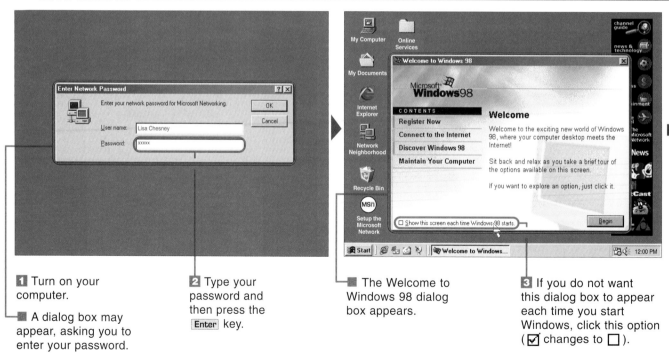

1 Turn on your computer.

■ A dialog box may appear, asking you to enter your password.

2 Type your password and then press the `Enter` key.

■ The Welcome to Windows 98 dialog box appears.

3 If you do not want this dialog box to appear each time you start Windows, click this option (☑ changes to ☐).

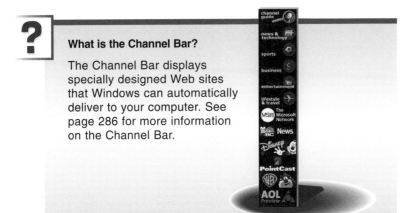

? **What is the Channel Bar?**

The Channel Bar displays specially designed Web sites that Windows can automatically deliver to your computer. See page 286 for more information on the Channel Bar.

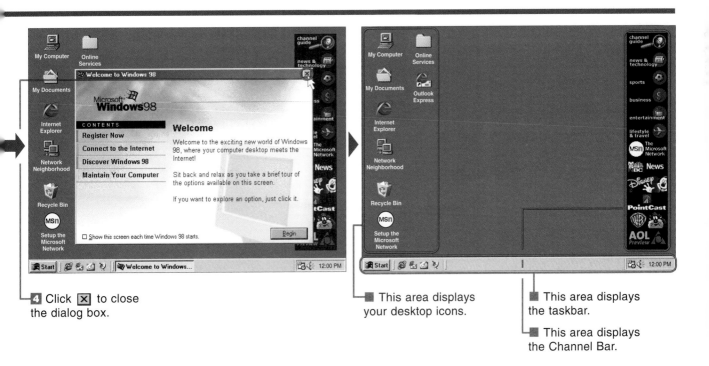

4 Click ☒ to close the dialog box.

■ This area displays your desktop icons.

■ This area displays the taskbar.

■ This area displays the Channel Bar.

START A PROGRAM

You can use the
Start button to start
your programs.

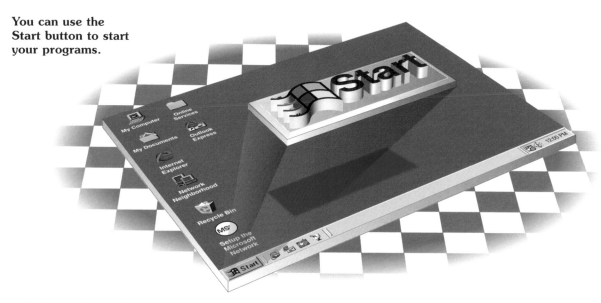

START A PROGRAM

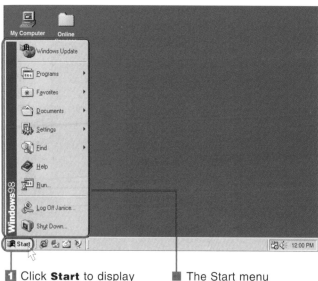

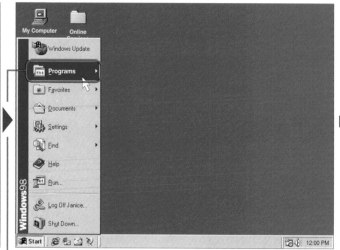

1 Click **Start** to display
the Start menu.

*Note: To display the Start menu
using the keyboard, press and
hold down the* Ctrl *key and
then press the* Esc *key.*

■ The Start menu
appears.

2 Click **Programs** to
display the programs
available on your
computer.

*Note: To select a menu item
using the keyboard, press the
key for the underlined letter
(example:* **P** *for* **P***rograms).*

Which programs does Windows provide?

Windows comes with many useful programs.

WordPad is a word processing program that lets you create letters, reports and memos.

Paint is a drawing program that lets you draw pictures and maps.

ScanDisk is a program that searches for and repairs disk errors.

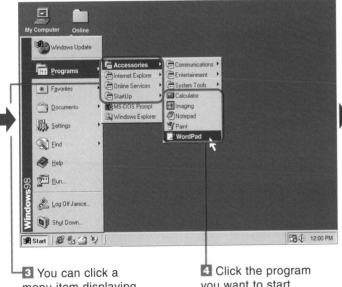

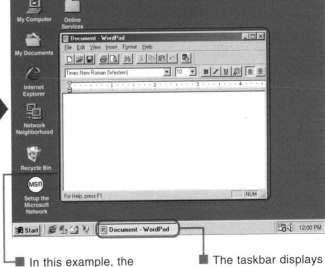

3 You can click a menu item displaying an arrow (▶) to view additional programs (example: **Accessories**).

4 Click the program you want to start (example: **WordPad**).

Note: To close the Start menu without selecting a program, click outside the menu area or press the **Alt** *key.*

■ In this example, the WordPad window appears.

■ The taskbar displays a button for the open window.

MAXIMIZE A WINDOW

You can enlarge a
window to fill your
screen. This lets you
view more of the
window's contents.

MAXIMIZE A WINDOW

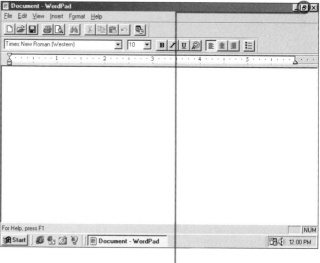

1 Click 🗖 in the window
you want to maximize.

■ The window fills
your screen.

■ To return the window to
its previous size, click 🗗.

If you are not using a window, you can minimize the window to remove it from your screen. You can redisplay the window at any time.

MINIMIZE A WINDOW

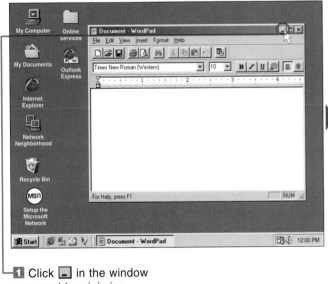

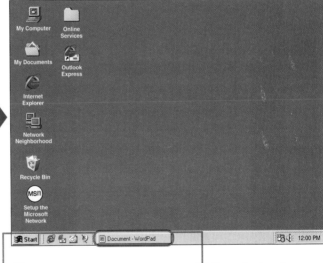

1 Click ▬ in the window you want to minimize.

■ The window reduces to a button on the taskbar.

■ To redisplay the window, click its button on the taskbar.

MOVE A WINDOW

If a window covers items
on your screen, you can
move the window to a
different location.

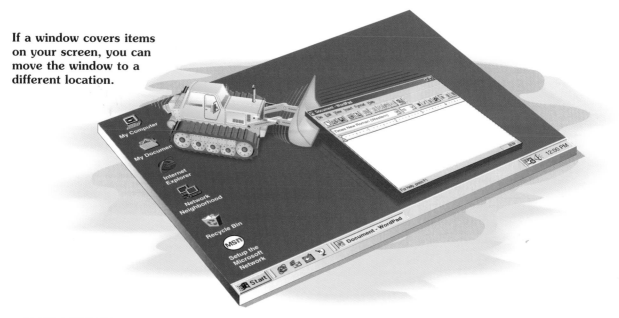

MOVE A WINDOW

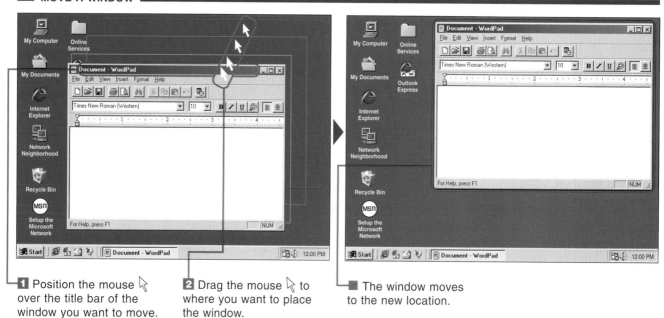

1 Position the mouse ▷
over the title bar of the
window you want to move.

2 Drag the mouse ▷ to
where you want to place
the window.

■ The window moves
to the new location.

You can easily change the size of a window displayed on your screen.

Enlarging a window lets you view more of its contents. Reducing a window lets you view items covered by the window.

SIZE A WINDOW

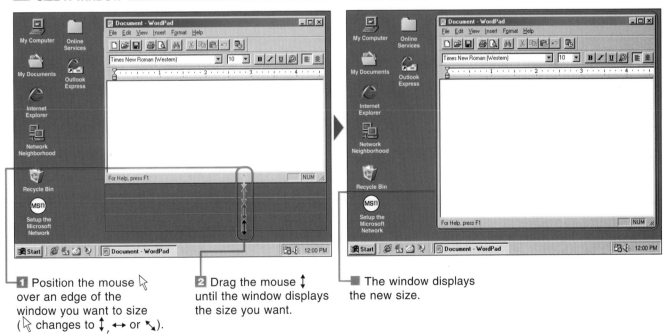

1 Position the mouse ⌐ over an edge of the window you want to size (⌐ changes to ↕, ↔ or ⤡).

2 Drag the mouse ↕ until the window displays the size you want.

■ The window displays the new size.

SCROLL THROUGH A WINDOW

You can use a scroll bar to browse through the information in a window. This is useful when a window is not large enough to display all the information it contains.

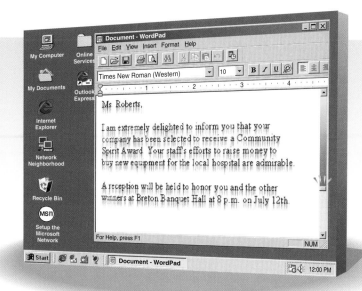

SCROLL DOWN

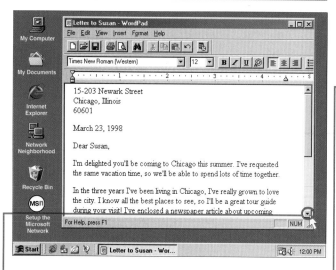

1 Click ▼ to scroll down through the information in a window.

SCROLL UP

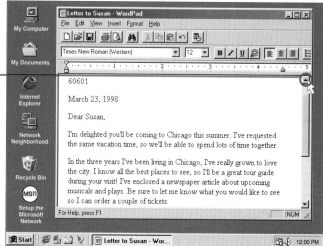

1 Click ▲ to scroll up through the information in a window.

Is there another way to use a mouse to scroll through a window?

You can purchase a mouse with a wheel between the left and right mouse buttons. Moving this wheel lets you scroll through a window.

SCROLL TO ANY POSITION

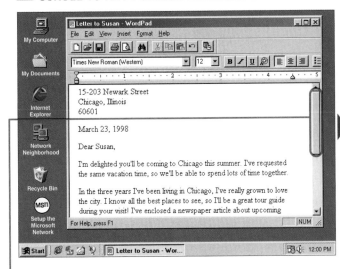

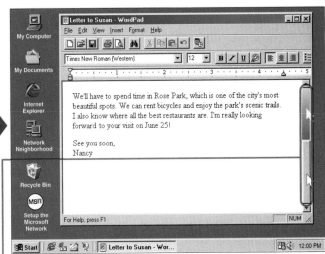

■ The location of the scroll box indicates which part of the window you are viewing. For example, when the scroll box is halfway down the scroll bar, you are viewing information from the middle of the window.

Note: The size of the scroll box varies, depending on the amount of information the window contains.

1 Drag the scroll box along the scroll bar until the information you want to view appears.

SWITCH BETWEEN WINDOWS

You can have more than one
window open at a time.
You can easily switch
between all the
windows you
have open.

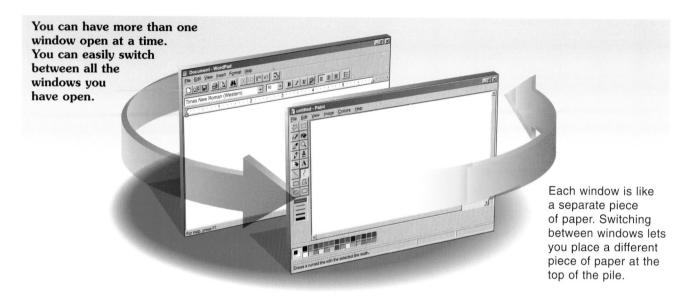

Each window is like
a separate piece
of paper. Switching
between windows lets
you place a different
piece of paper at the
top of the pile.

SWITCH BETWEEN WINDOWS

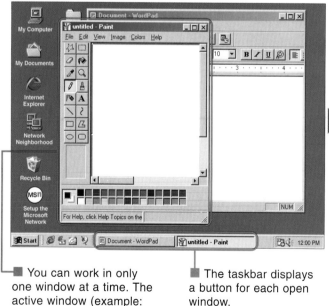

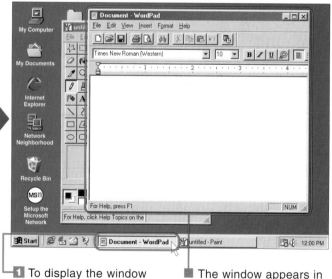

■ You can work in only
one window at a time. The
active window (example:
Paint) appears in front of
all other windows and
displays a blue title bar.

■ The taskbar displays
a button for each open
window.

1 To display the window
you want to work with in
front of all other windows,
click its button on the
taskbar.

■ The window appears in
front of all other windows.
This lets you clearly view
the contents of the window.

CLOSE A WINDOW

When you finish working with a window, you can close the window to remove it from your screen.

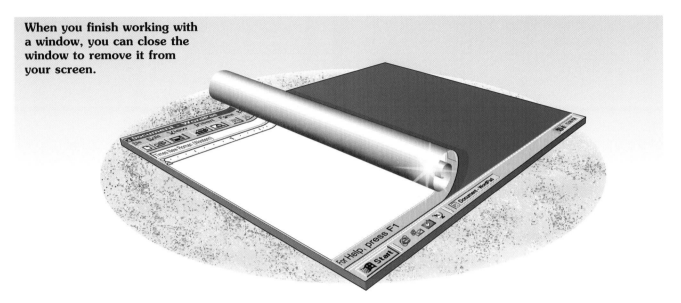

■ CLOSE A WINDOW ■

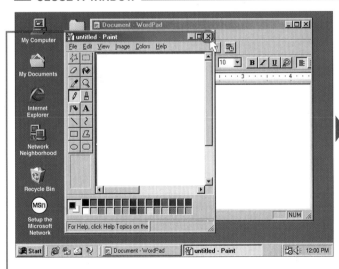

1 Click ⊠ in the window you want to close.

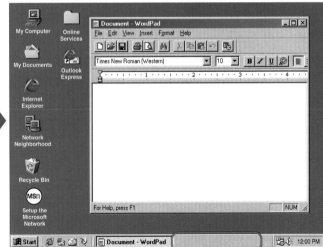

■ The window disappears from your screen.

■ The button for the window disappears from the taskbar.

ARRANGE WINDOWS

If you have several windows open, some of them may be hidden from view. The Cascade feature lets you display your open windows one on top of the other.

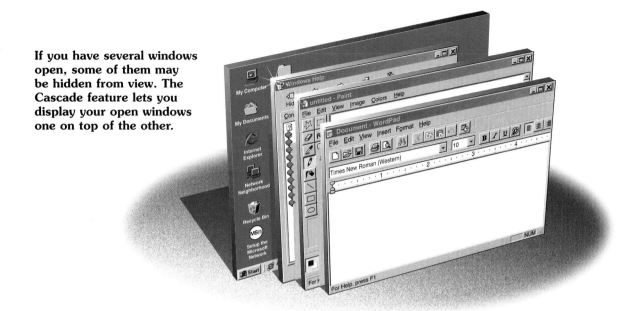

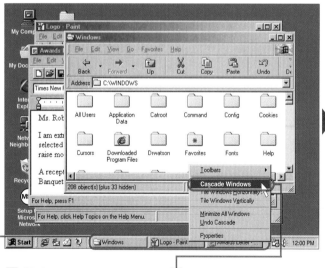

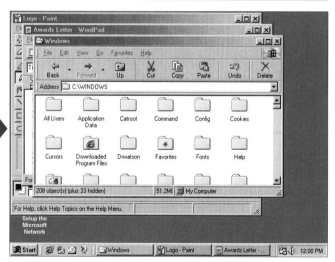

1 Click an empty area on the taskbar using the **right** mouse button. A menu appears.

2 Click **Cascade Windows**.

■ The windows neatly overlap each other.

You can use the Tile
feature to view the
contents of all your
open windows at once.

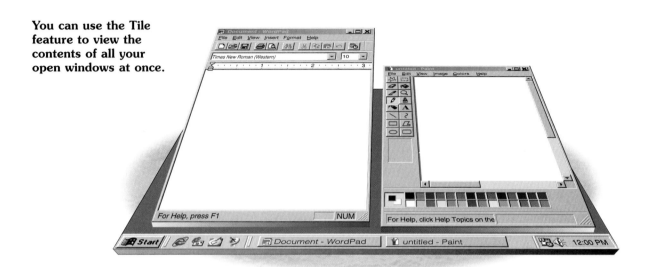

TILE WINDOWS

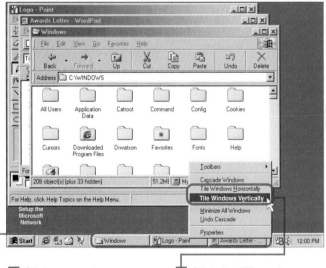

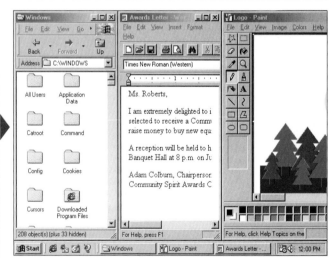

1 Click an empty area
on the taskbar using the
right mouse button. A
menu appears.

2 Click the Tile option
you want to use.

■ You can now view
the contents of all your
open windows.

SHOW THE DESKTOP

You can instantly minimize all your open windows to remove them from your screen. This allows you to clearly view the desktop.

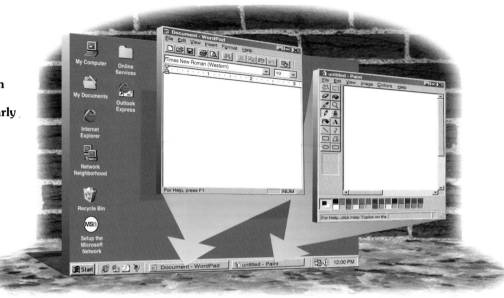

SHOW THE DESKTOP

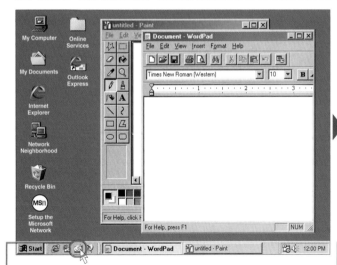

1 Click ✎ to minimize all the open windows on your screen.

■ Each window minimizes to a button on the taskbar. You can now clearly view the desktop.

■ To redisplay a window, click its button on the taskbar.

22

When you finish using
your computer, shut
down Windows before
turning off the computer.

■ Do not turn off your
computer until this
message appears on
your screen.

SHUT DOWN WINDOWS

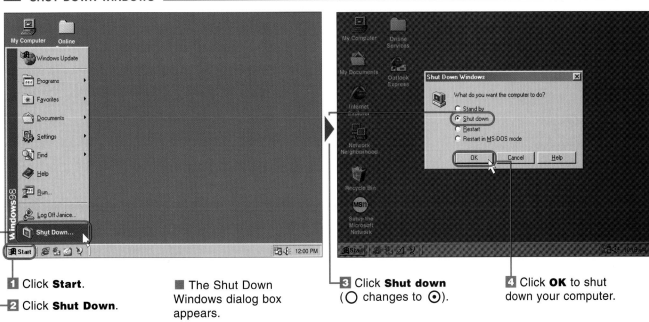

1 Click **Start**.

2 Click **Shut Down**.

■ The Shut Down
Windows dialog box
appears.

3 Click **Shut down**
(○ changes to ⊙).

4 Click **OK** to shut
down your computer.

GETTING HELP

If you do not know how to perform a task, you can use the Help feature to get information.

HELP DESK

GETTING HELP

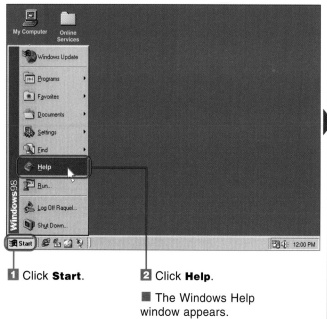

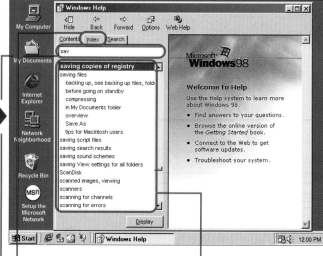

1 Click **Start**.

2 Click **Help**.

■ The Windows Help window appears.

3 Click the **Index** tab to display an alphabetical list of help topics.

4 To search for a help topic of interest, click this area and then type the first few letters of the topic.

■ This area displays help topics beginning with the letters you typed.

? How can I use the Help feature to find information on a topic of interest?

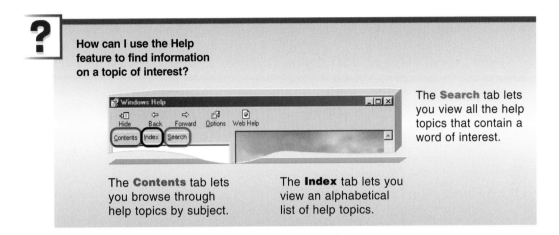

The **Search** tab lets you view all the help topics that contain a word of interest.

The **Contents** tab lets you browse through help topics by subject.

The **Index** tab lets you view an alphabetical list of help topics.

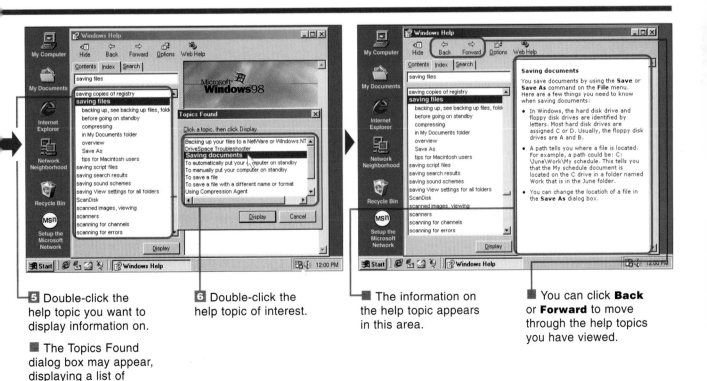

5 Double-click the help topic you want to display information on.

■ The Topics Found dialog box may appear, displaying a list of related help topics.

6 Double-click the help topic of interest.

■ The information on the help topic appears in this area.

■ You can click **Back** or **Forward** to move through the help topics you have viewed.

USING THE CALCULATOR

Windows provides a
calculator you can
use to perform
calculations.

USING THE CALCULATOR

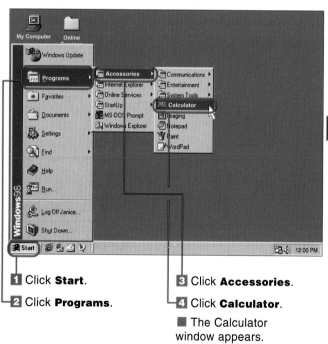

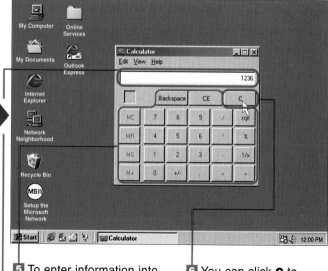

1 Click **Start**.

2 Click **Programs**.

3 Click **Accessories**.

4 Click **Calculator**.

■ The Calculator
window appears.

5 To enter information into
the Calculator, click each
button as you would press
the buttons on a handheld
calculator.

■ This area displays the
numbers you enter and the
result of each calculation.

6 You can click **C** to
start a new calculation
at any time.

26

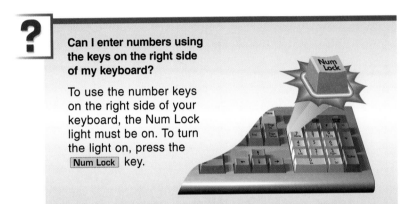

Can I enter numbers using the keys on the right side of my keyboard?

To use the number keys on the right side of your keyboard, the Num Lock light must be on. To turn the light on, press the Num Lock key.

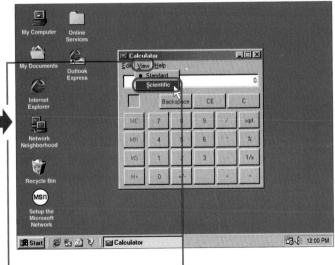

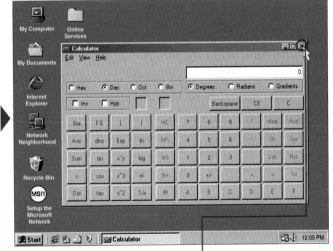

7 To change to the Scientific view of the Calculator, click **View**.

8 Click **Scientific**.

■ The Scientific view of the Calculator appears. You can use this view to perform more complex calculations, such as averages and exponents.

Note: To return to the Standard view, perform steps 7 and 8, selecting Standard in step 8.

9 When you finish using the Calculator, click ✕ to close the Calculator window.

CHAPTER 2

Create Documents

In this chapter you will learn how to use the WordPad program. WordPad allows you to create documents, such as letters and memos, quickly and efficiently.

Dear Kevin:

START WORDPAD

WordPad allows you to create simple documents, such as letters and memos.

START WORDPAD

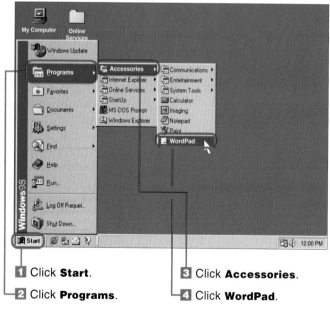

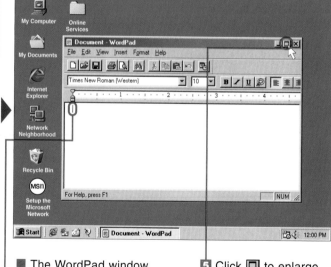

1 Click **Start**.

2 Click **Programs**.

3 Click **Accessories**.

4 Click **WordPad**.

■ The WordPad window appears with a new, blank document.

■ The flashing line on your screen, called the insertion point, indicates where the text you type will appear.

5 Click 🔲 to enlarge the WordPad window to fill your screen.

Does WordPad offer all the features I need?

WordPad is a simple program that offers only basic word processing features. If you need more advanced features, you can purchase a more powerful word processor, such as Microsoft Word or Corel WordPerfect. These programs include features, such as tables, graphics, a spell checker and a thesaurus.

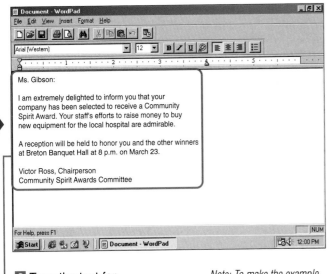

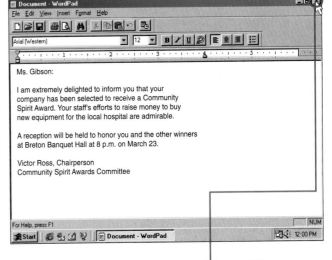

6 Type the text for your document.

■ When you reach the end of a line, WordPad automatically moves the text to the next line. You only need to press the Enter key when you want to start a new line or paragraph.

Note: To make the example easier to read, the font type and size have been changed. To change the font type and size, see pages 40 and 41.

When you finish using WordPad, you can exit the program.

1 Before exiting WordPad, save any changes you made to the document. To save your changes, see page 36.

2 Click ☒ to exit WordPad.

EDIT TEXT

You can easily add new text to your document and remove text you no longer need.

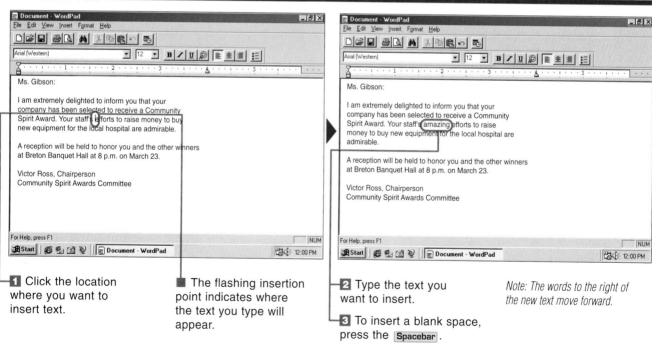

INSERT TEXT

1 Click the location where you want to insert text.

■ The flashing insertion point indicates where the text you type will appear.

2 Type the text you want to insert.

3 To insert a blank space, press the Spacebar.

Note: The words to the right of the new text move forward.

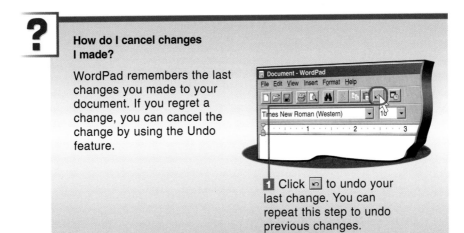

?

How do I cancel changes I made?

WordPad remembers the last changes you made to your document. If you regret a change, you can cancel the change by using the Undo feature.

1 Click ↶ to undo your last change. You can repeat this step to undo previous changes.

DELETE TEXT

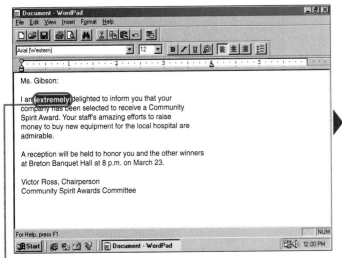

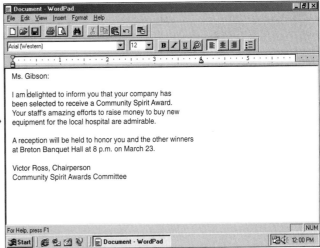

1 To select the text you want to delete, drag the mouse I over the text until the text is highlighted.

2 Press the Delete key to remove the text.

■ To delete one character at a time, click to the left of the first character you want to delete. Press the Delete key for each character you want to remove.

MOVE TEXT

You can reorganize your document by moving text from one location to another.

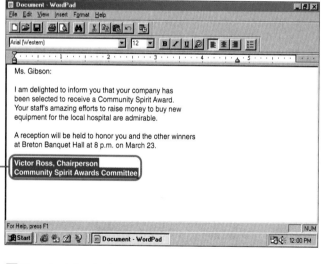

1 To select the text you want to move, drag the mouse I over the text until the text is highlighted.

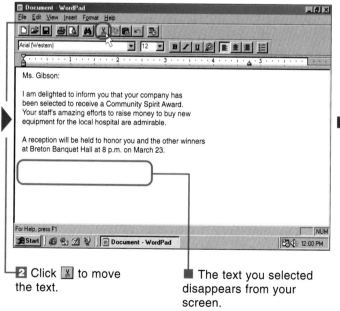

2 Click ✂ to move the text.

■ The text you selected disappears from your screen.

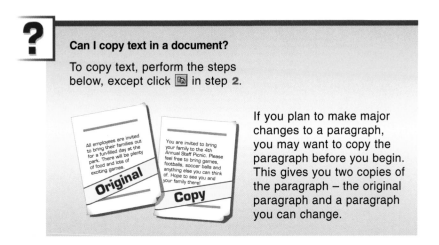

Can I copy text in a document?

To copy text, perform the steps below, except click 🖺 in step **2**.

If you plan to make major changes to a paragraph, you may want to copy the paragraph before you begin. This gives you two copies of the paragraph – the original paragraph and a paragraph you can change.

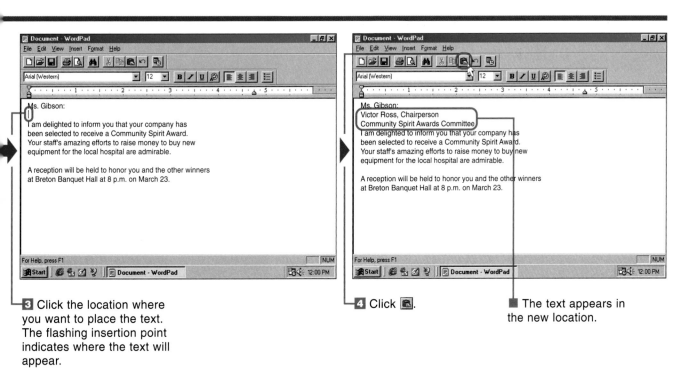

3 Click the location where you want to place the text. The flashing insertion point indicates where the text will appear.

4 Click 🖺.

■ The text appears in the new location.

SAVE A DOCUMENT

You should save your document to store it for future use. This lets you later retrieve the document for reviewing or editing.

You should regularly save changes you make to a document to avoid losing your work.

◼ SAVE A DOCUMENT ◼

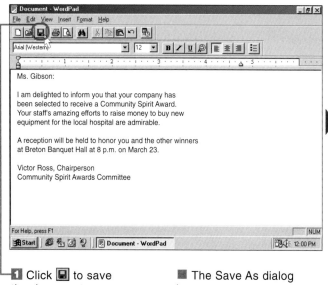

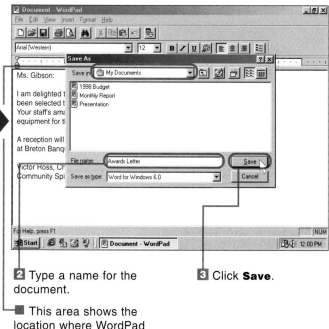

1 Click 🖫 to save the document.

◼ The Save As dialog box appears.

Note: If you previously saved the document, the Save As dialog box will not appear since you have already named the document.

2 Type a name for the document.

◼ This area shows the location where WordPad will store the document.

3 Click **Save**.

You can produce a
paper copy of the
document displayed
on your screen.

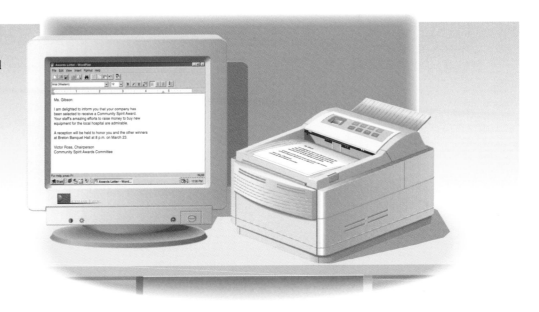

PRINT A DOCUMENT

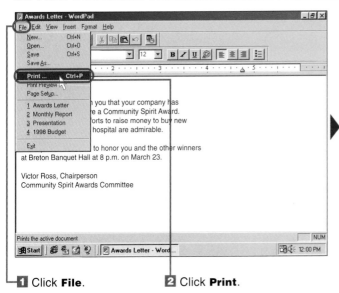

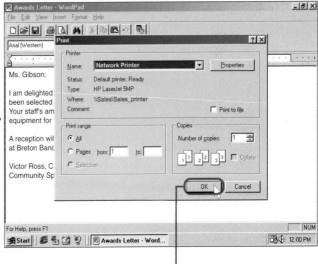

1 Click **File**.

2 Click **Print**.

■ The Print dialog
box appears.

3 Click **OK** to print
the document.

OPEN A DOCUMENT

You can open a saved
document and display the
document on your screen.
This allows you to view
and make changes to the
document.

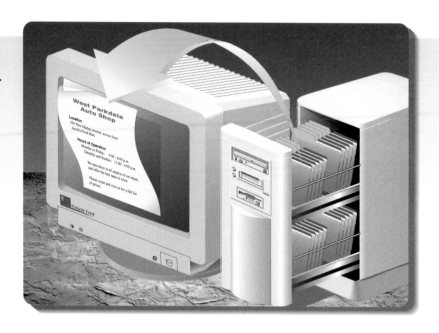

OPEN A DOCUMENT

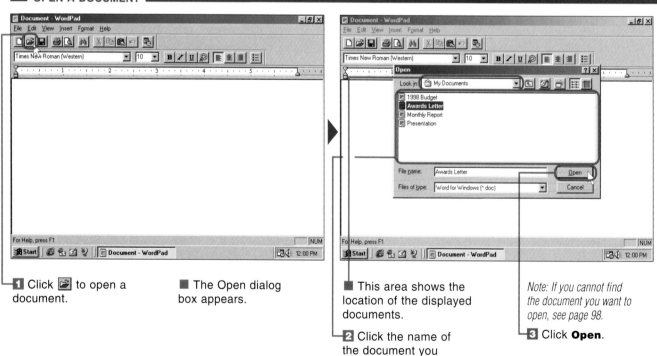

1 Click 🗁 to open a
document.

■ The Open dialog
box appears.

■ This area shows the
location of the displayed
documents.

2 Click the name of
the document you
want to open.

*Note: If you cannot find
the document you want to
open, see page 98.*

3 Click **Open**.

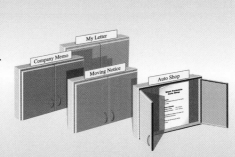

Can I work with two WordPad documents at the same time?

WordPad only lets you work with one document at a time. If you are currently working with a document, save the document before opening another. For information on saving a document, see page 36.

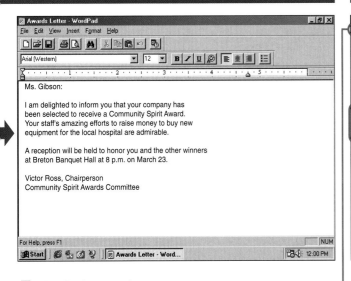

■ WordPad opens the document and displays it on your screen. You can now review and make changes to the document.

QUICKLY OPEN A DOCUMENT

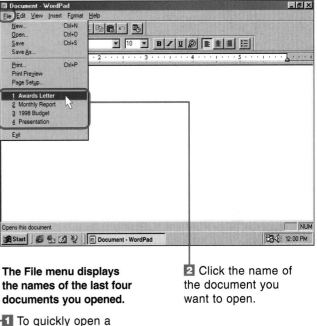

The File menu displays the names of the last four documents you opened.

1 To quickly open a document, click **File**.

2 Click the name of the document you want to open.

CHANGE FONT TYPE

You can enhance the
appearance of your
document by changing
the design of the text.

CHANGE FONT TYPE

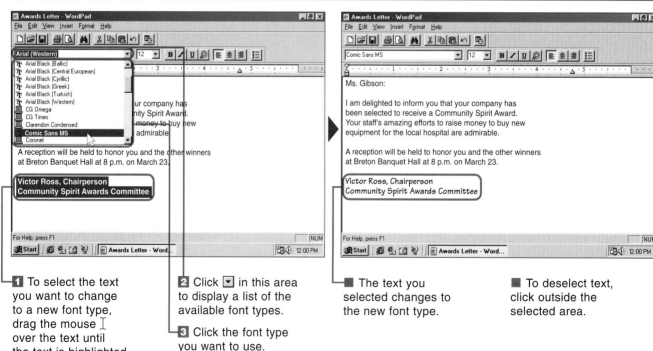

1 To select the text
you want to change
to a new font type,
drag the mouse I
over the text until
the text is highlighted.

2 Click ▼ in this area
to display a list of the
available font types.

3 Click the font type
you want to use.

■ The text you
selected changes to
the new font type.

■ To deselect text,
click outside the
selected area.

You can increase or
decrease the size of
text in your document.

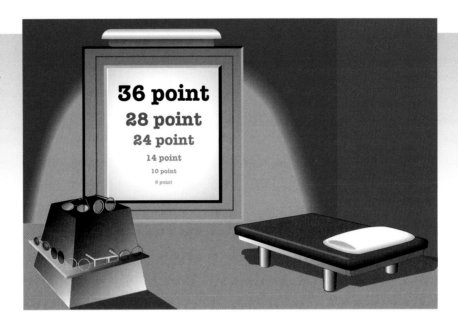

CHANGE FONT SIZE

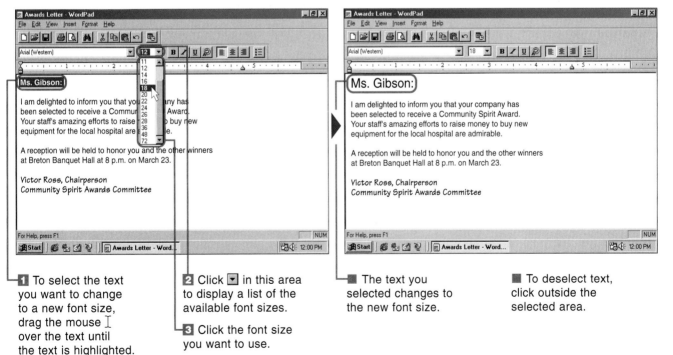

1 To select the text
you want to change
to a new font size,
drag the mouse I
over the text until
the text is highlighted.

2 Click ▼ in this area
to display a list of the
available font sizes.

3 Click the font size
you want to use.

■ The text you
selected changes to
the new font size.

■ To deselect text,
click outside the
selected area.

BOLD, ITALIC AND UNDERLINE

You can use the Bold, Italic and Underline features to emphasize important information in your document.

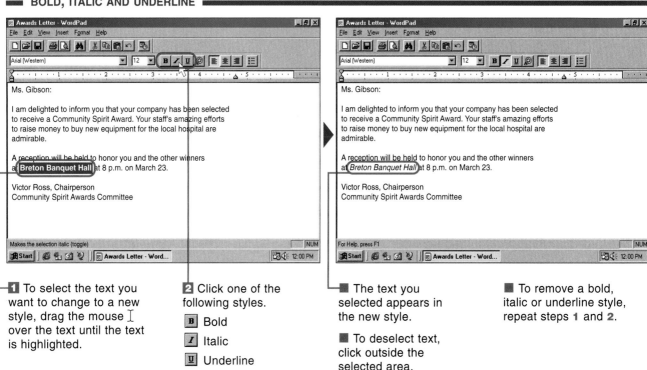

1 To select the text you want to change to a new style, drag the mouse I over the text until the text is highlighted.

2 Click one of the following styles.

B Bold

I Italic

U Underline

■ The text you selected appears in the new style.

■ To deselect text, click outside the selected area.

■ To remove a bold, italic or underline style, repeat steps **1** and **2**.

You can make your document look more attractive by aligning text in different ways.

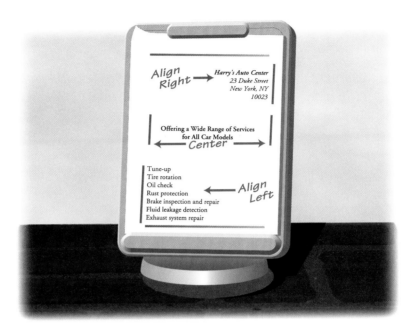

CHANGE ALIGNMENT OF TEXT

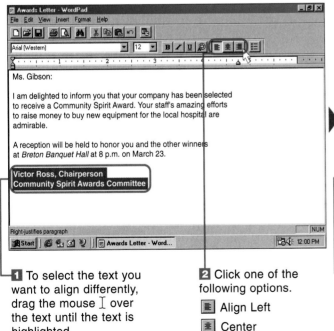

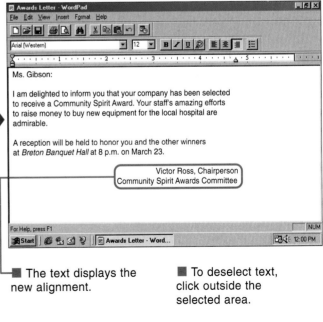

1 To select the text you want to align differently, drag the mouse I over the text until the text is highlighted.

2 Click one of the following options.

📧 Align Left

📧 Center

📧 Align Right

■ The text displays the new alignment.

■ To deselect text, click outside the selected area.

CHAPTER 3

Create Pictures

This chapter will show you how to use Paint to create, save, open and print your pictures, as well as how to use a picture as your desktop background.

START PAINT

You can use Paint to
draw pictures and maps
on your computer.

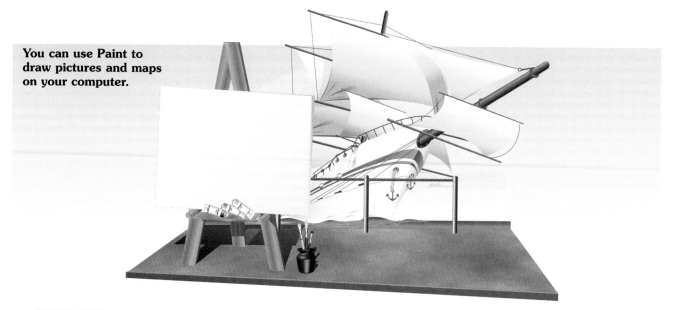

START PAINT

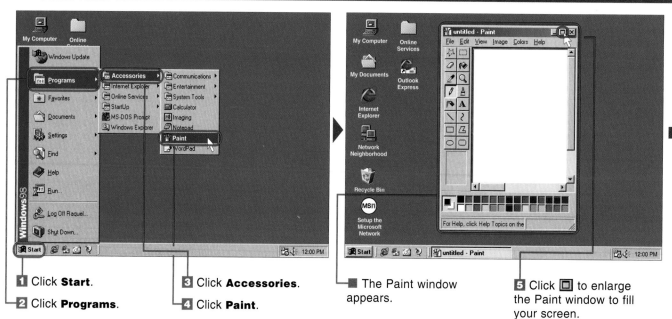

1 Click **Start**.

2 Click **Programs**.

3 Click **Accessories**.

4 Click **Paint**.

■ The Paint window
appears.

5 Click ▣ to enlarge
the Paint window to fill
your screen.

46

What can I do with the pictures I draw in Paint?

You can place the pictures you draw in Paint in other programs. For example, you can add your company logo to a business letter you created in WordPad.

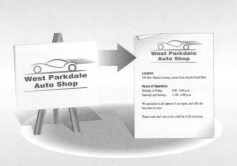

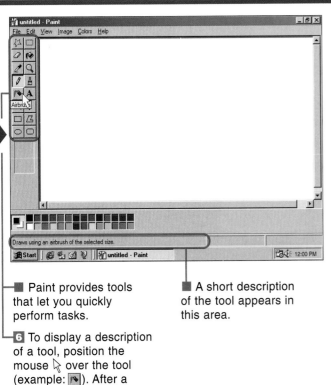

■ Paint provides tools that let you quickly perform tasks.

■ A short description of the tool appears in this area.

6 To display a description of a tool, position the mouse ⊳ over the tool (example: ▨). After a moment, the name of the tool appears.

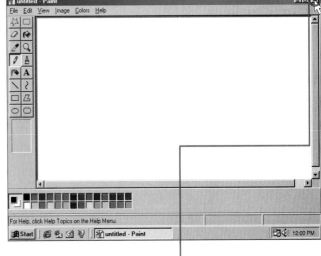

You can exit Paint when you finish using the program.

1 Before exiting Paint, save any changes you made to the picture. To save your changes, see page 55.

2 Click ✕ to exit Paint.

DRAW SHAPES

You can draw shapes such as circles and squares in various colors.

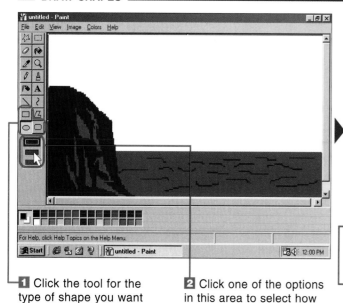

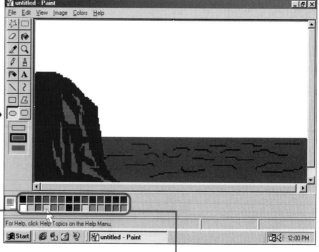

1 Click the tool for the type of shape you want to draw (example: ⬭).

2 Click one of the options in this area to select how you want to draw the shape.

Note: For more information, see the top of page 49.

3 To select a color for the outline of the shape, click the color (example: ■).

4 To select a color for the inside of the shape, click the color using the **right** mouse button (example: □).

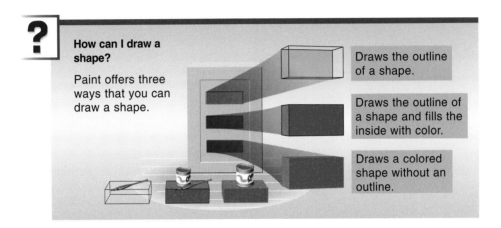

How can I draw a shape?

Paint offers three ways that you can draw a shape.

Draws the outline of a shape.

Draws the outline of a shape and fills the inside with color.

Draws a colored shape without an outline.

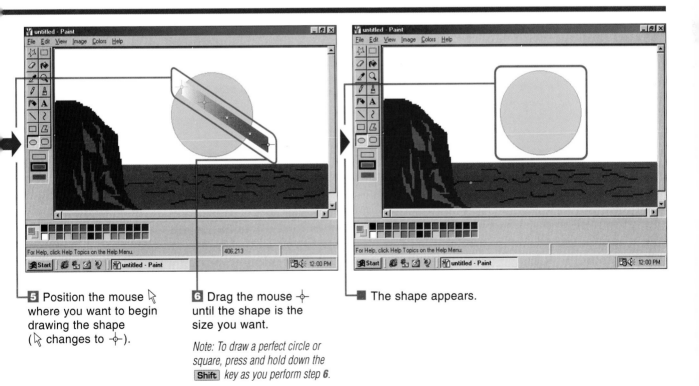

5 Position the mouse ⬡ where you want to begin drawing the shape (⬡ changes to ✛).

6 Drag the mouse ✛ until the shape is the size you want.

Note: To draw a perfect circle or square, press and hold down the **Shift** *key as you perform step* **6**.

■ The shape appears.

DRAW LINES

You can draw
straight, wavy
and curved lines
in various colors.

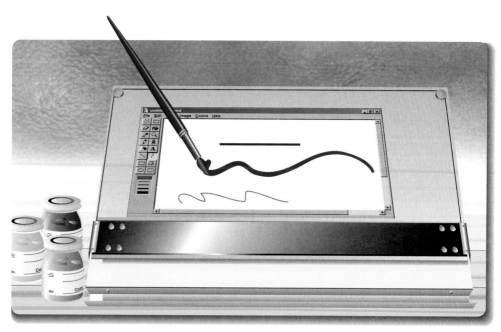

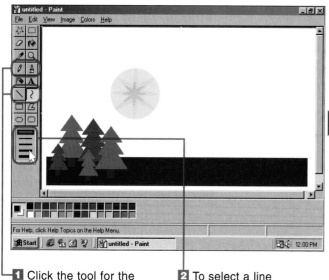

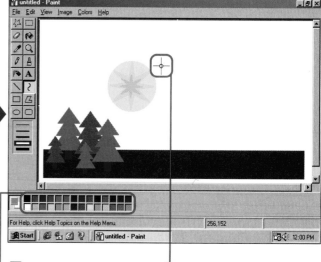

1 Click the tool for the
type of line you want to
draw (example: ▨).

*Note: For more information,
see the top of page 51.*

2 To select a line
thickness, click one of
the options in this area.

*Note: The ▨ tool does not
provide any line thickness
options. The ▨ tool provides
a different set of options.*

3 To select a color
for the line, click the
color (example: ▨).

4 Position the mouse ▨
where you want to begin
drawing the line (▨ changes
to ✛, ✐ or ✛).

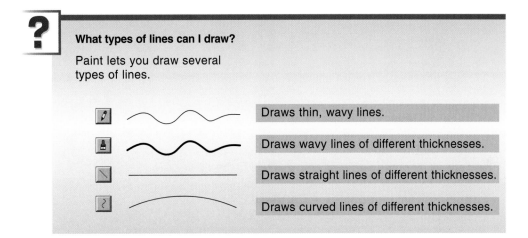

What types of lines can I draw?

Paint lets you draw several types of lines.

Draws thin, wavy lines.

Draws wavy lines of different thicknesses.

Draws straight lines of different thicknesses.

Draws curved lines of different thicknesses.

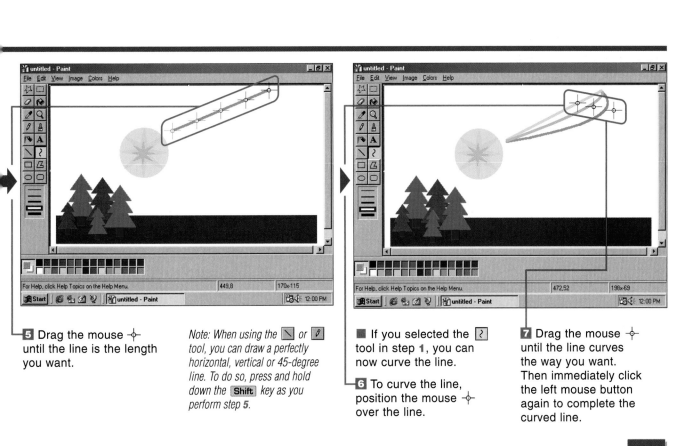

5 Drag the mouse -⊕- until the line is the length you want.

Note: When using the ◻ or ◻ tool, you can draw a perfectly horizontal, vertical or 45-degree line. To do so, press and hold down the Shift *key as you perform step 5.*

■ If you selected the ◻ tool in step **1**, you can now curve the line.

6 To curve the line, position the mouse -⊕- over the line.

7 Drag the mouse -⊕- until the line curves the way you want. Then immediately click the left mouse button again to complete the curved line.

ADD TEXT

You can add text to
your picture, such as
a title or explanation.

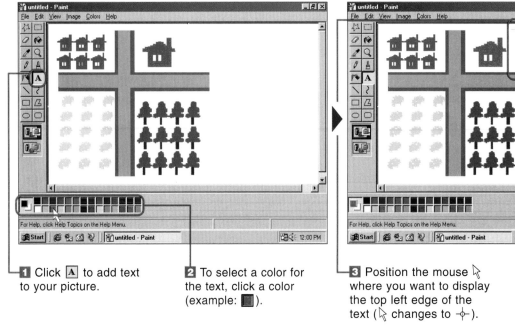

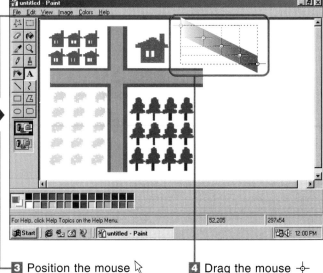

1 Click **A** to add text
to your picture.

2 To select a color for
the text, click a color
(example: ■).

3 Position the mouse ▷
where you want to display
the top left edge of the
text (▷ changes to ╬).

4 Drag the mouse ╬
to select the area where
you want the text to
appear.

■ A dotted box appears.

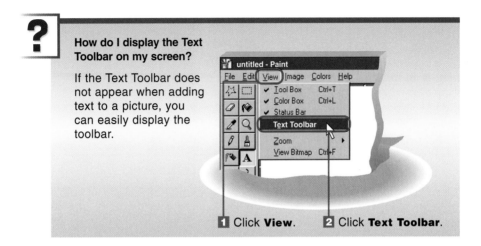

How do I display the Text Toolbar on my screen?

If the Text Toolbar does not appear when adding text to a picture, you can easily display the toolbar.

1 Click **View**.　　**2** Click **Text Toolbar**.

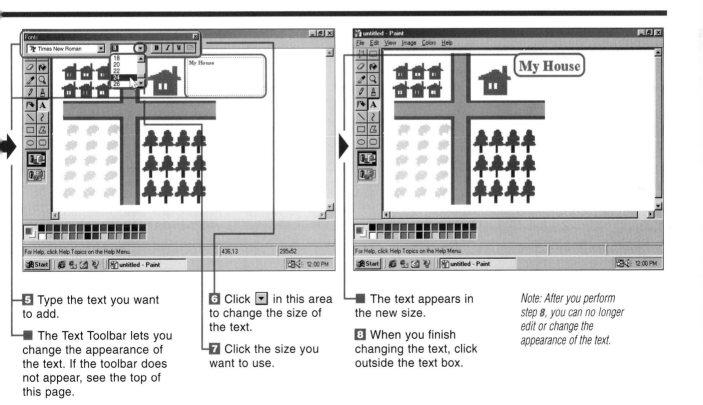

5 Type the text you want to add.

■ The Text Toolbar lets you change the appearance of the text. If the toolbar does not appear, see the top of this page.

6 Click ▼ in this area to change the size of the text.

7 Click the size you want to use.

■ The text appears in the new size.

8 When you finish changing the text, click outside the text box.

Note: After you perform step 8, you can no longer edit or change the appearance of the text.

ERASE PART OF A PICTURE

You can use the
Eraser tool to
remove part of
your picture.

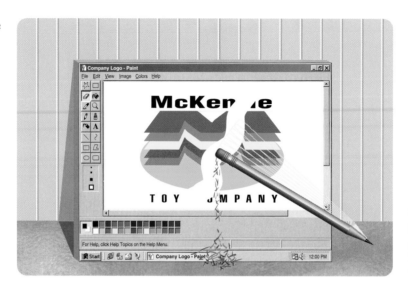

When choosing a color
for the eraser, select
a color that matches
the background color
of your picture.

ERASE PART OF A PICTURE

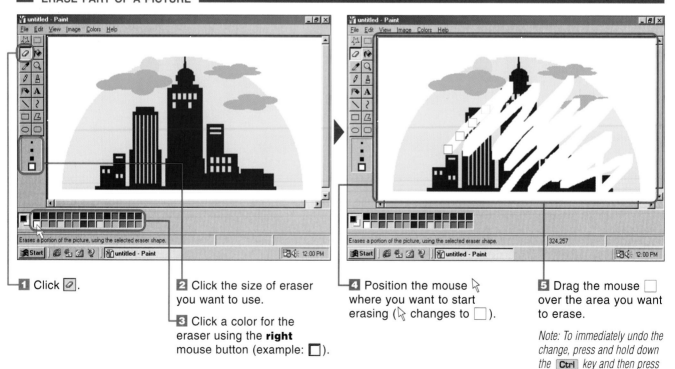

1 Click .

2 Click the size of eraser
you want to use.

3 Click a color for the
eraser using the **right**
mouse button (example: ☐).

4 Position the mouse ↖
where you want to start
erasing (↖ changes to ☐).

5 Drag the mouse ☐
over the area you want
to erase.

*Note: To immediately undo the
change, press and hold down
the* `Ctrl` *key and then press
the* `Z` *key.*

You should save
your picture to
store it for future
use. This allows
you to later review
and make changes
to the picture.

You should regularly
save changes you
make to a picture
to avoid losing
your work.

■ SAVE A PICTURE ■

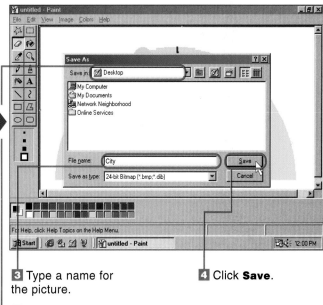

-1 Click **File**.

-2 Click **Save**.

■ The Save As dialog
box appears.

*Note: If you previously saved
the picture, the Save As dialog
box will not appear since you
have already named the picture.*

3 Type a name for
the picture.

■ This area shows the
location where Paint will
store the picture.

4 Click **Save**.

OPEN A PICTURE

You can open a saved picture and display the picture on your screen. This allows you to view and make changes to the picture.

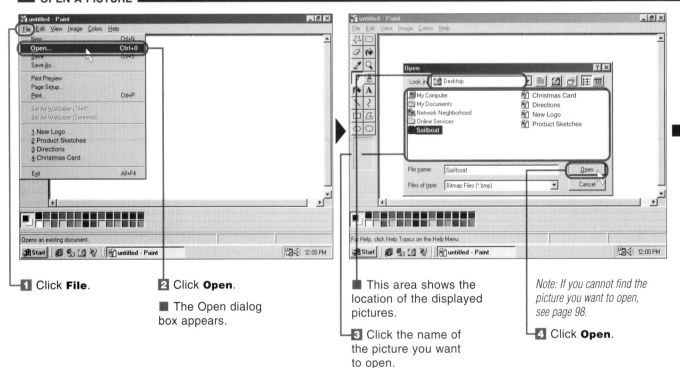

OPEN A PICTURE

1 Click **File**.

2 Click **Open**.

■ The Open dialog box appears.

■ This area shows the location of the displayed pictures.

3 Click the name of the picture you want to open.

Note: If you cannot find the picture you want to open, see page 98.

4 Click **Open**.

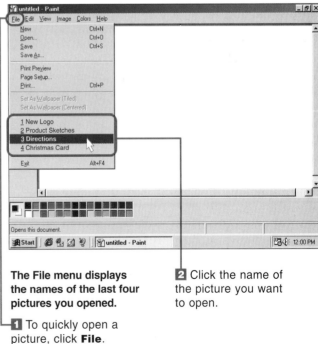

Can I work with two pictures at the same time?

Paint lets you work with only one picture at a time. If you are currently working with a picture, save the picture before opening another. For information on saving a picture, see page 55.

QUICKLY OPEN A PICTURE

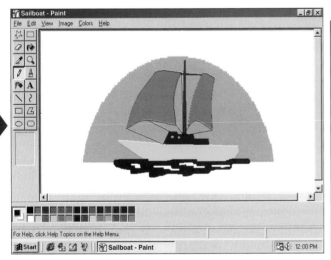

■ Paint opens the picture and displays it on your screen. You can now review and make changes to the picture.

The File menu displays the names of the last four pictures you opened.

1 To quickly open a picture, click **File**.

2 Click the name of the picture you want to open.

PRINT A PICTURE

You can produce
a paper copy of a
picture you created.

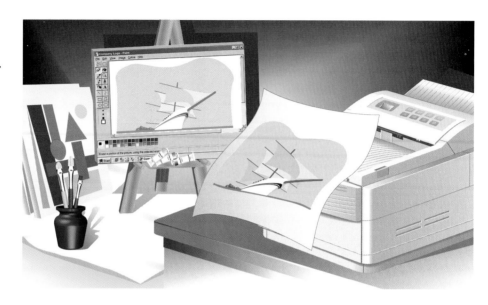

PRINT A PICTURE

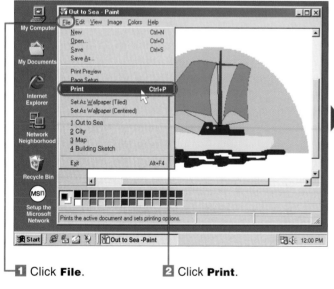

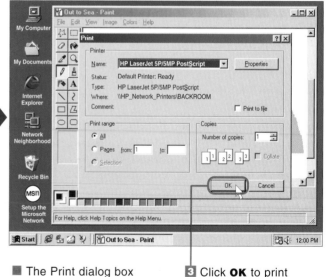

1 Click **File**.

2 Click **Print**.

■ The Print dialog box
appears.

3 Click **OK** to print
the picture.

USE PICTURE AS DESKTOP BACKGROUND

You can use a picture as the background for your desktop.

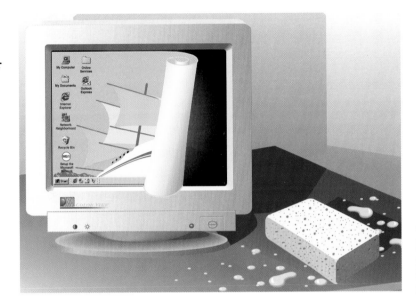

You must save a picture before you can use the picture as your desktop background. To save a picture, see page 55.

USE PICTURE AS DESKTOP BACKGROUND

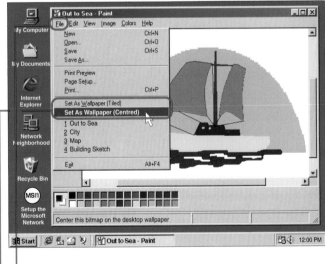

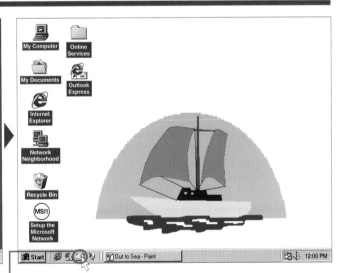

1 To use the displayed picture as your desktop background, click **File**.

2 Click the way you want the picture to appear on your desktop.

Tiled - Repeat picture to cover desktop.

Centered - Display picture centered on the desktop.

3 Click ☑ to minimize all open windows so you can clearly view the desktop.

■ The picture appears on your desktop.

■ To restore the original desktop background, see page 112.

CHAPTER 4

View Files

This chapter teaches you how to view the folders and files stored on your computer. You will also learn how to change the way Windows displays items on your screen.

VIEW CONTENTS OF YOUR COMPUTER

You can easily view the folders and files stored on your computer.

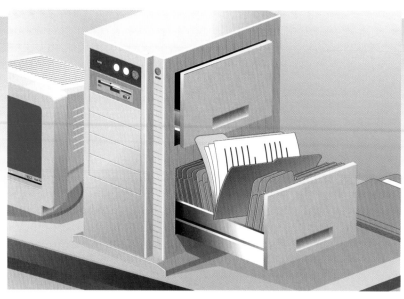

Like a filing cabinet, your computer uses folders to organize information.

VIEW CONTENTS OF YOUR COMPUTER

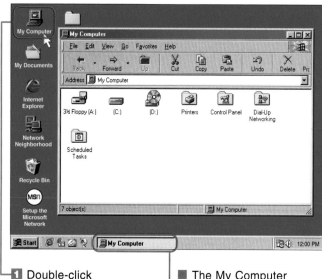

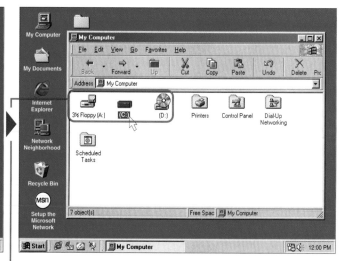

■1 Double-click **My Computer** to view the contents of your computer.

■ The My Computer window appears.

■ A button appears on the taskbar for the open window.

■ These items represent the drives on your computer.

■2 To display the contents of a drive, double-click the drive.

Note: If you want to view the contents of a floppy or CD-ROM drive, make sure you insert a floppy disk or CD-ROM disc before performing step 2.

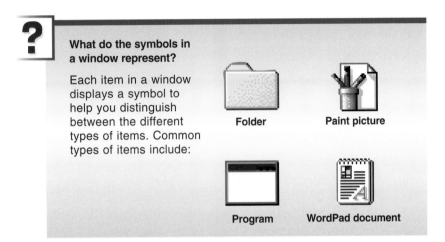

What do the symbols in a window represent?

Each item in a window displays a symbol to help you distinguish between the different types of items. Common types of items include:

Folder

Paint picture

Program

WordPad document

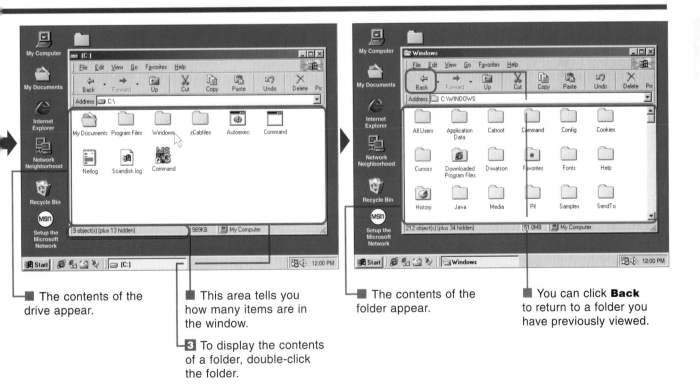

■ The contents of the drive appear.

■ This area tells you how many items are in the window.

3 To display the contents of a folder, double-click the folder.

■ The contents of the folder appear.

■ You can click **Back** to return to a folder you have previously viewed.

CHANGE APPEARANCE OF ITEMS

You can change the appearance of items in a window. Items can appear as large icons, small icons or in a list. You can also display details about each item.

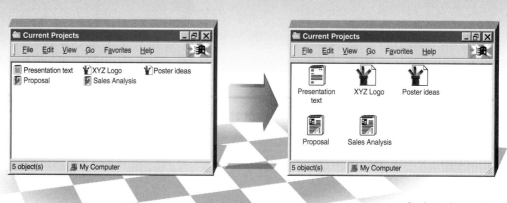

An icon is a picture that represents an item such as a file, folder or program.

CHANGE APPEARANCE OF ITEMS

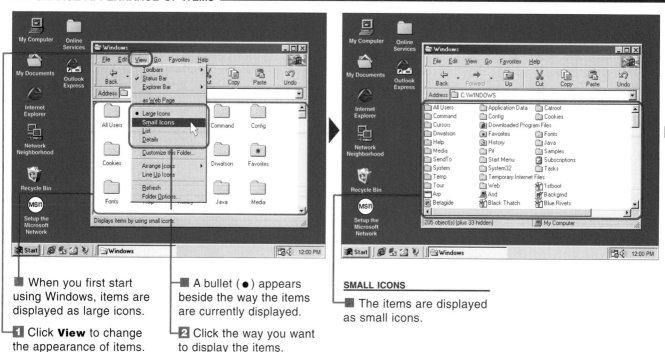

■ When you first start using Windows, items are displayed as large icons.

1 Click **View** to change the appearance of items.

■ A bullet (•) appears beside the way the items are currently displayed.

2 Click the way you want to display the items.

SMALL ICONS

■ The items are displayed as small icons.

64

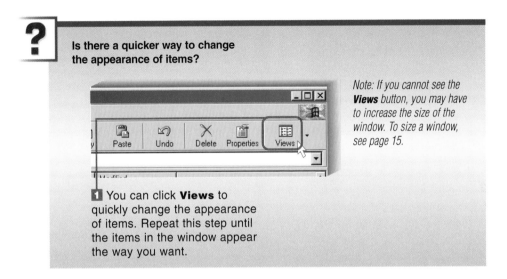

Note: If you cannot see the **Views** button, you may have to increase the size of the window. To size a window, see page 15.

? Is there a quicker way to change the appearance of items?

1 You can click **Views** to quickly change the appearance of items. Repeat this step until the items in the window appear the way you want.

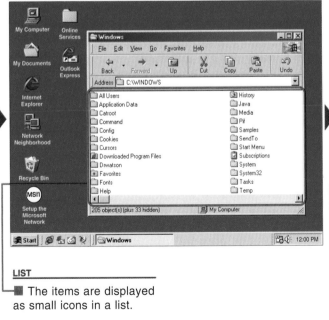

LIST

◼ The items are displayed as small icons in a list.

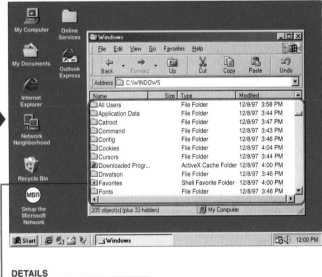

DETAILS

◼ Information about each item is displayed, such as the name, size and type of item.

SORT ITEMS

You can sort the items displayed in a window. This can help you find files and folders more easily.

NAME SORT ITEMS   SIZE SORT ITEMS   TYPE SORT ITEMS   DATE SORT ITEMS

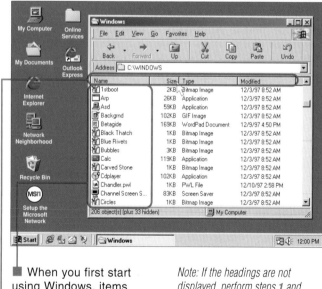

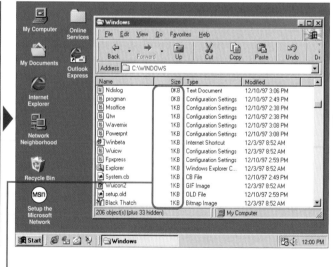

■ When you first start using Windows, items are sorted alphabetically by name.

*Note: If the headings are not displayed, perform steps 1 and 2 on page 64, selecting **Details** in step 2*

1 Click the heading for the column you want to use to sort the items.

■ To sort the items in reverse order, click the heading again.

SORT BY SIZE

■ The items are sorted by size.

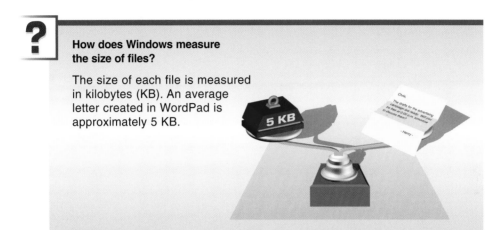

?

How does Windows measure the size of files?

The size of each file is measured in kilobytes (KB). An average letter created in WordPad is approximately 5 KB.

SORT BY TYPE

■ The items are sorted alphabetically by type.

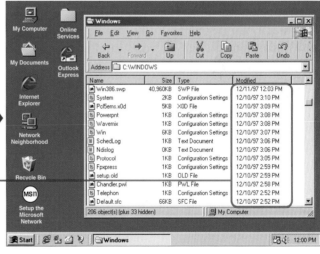

SORT BY DATE

■ The items are sorted by the date they were last saved.

ARRANGE ITEMS AUTOMATICALLY

You can have Windows automatically arrange items to fit neatly in a window.

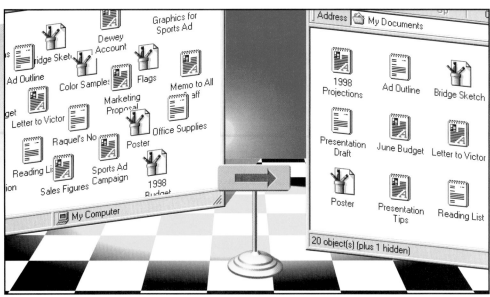

ARRANGE ITEMS AUTOMATICALLY

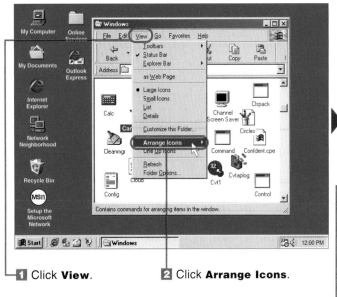

1 Click **View**.

2 Click **Arrange Icons**.

■ A check mark (✔) appears beside **Auto Arrange** when this feature is on.

3 Click **Auto Arrange** to turn this feature on.

*Note: If a check mark (✔) appears beside **Auto Arrange** and you want to leave this feature on, press the* Alt *key to close the menu.*

Why is the Auto Arrange feature not available?

The Auto Arrange feature is not available when items appear in the List or Details view. For information on changing the appearance of items, see page 64.

■ The items are automatically arranged in the window.

■ To turn off the Auto Arrange feature, repeat steps **1** to **3**.

■ When you change the size of a window and the Auto Arrange feature is on, Windows automatically rearranges the items to fit the new window size.

Note: To size a window, see page 15.

USING WINDOWS EXPLORER

Windows Explorer shows the location of every folder and file on your computer.

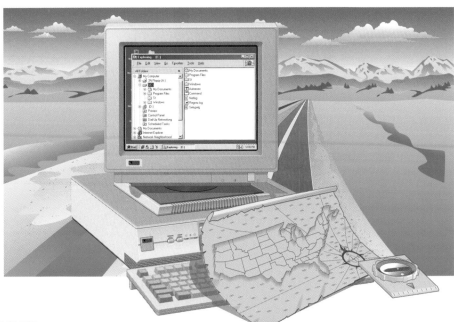

USING WINDOWS EXPLORER

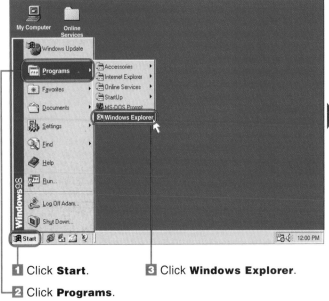

1 Click **Start**.

2 Click **Programs**.

3 Click **Windows Explorer**.

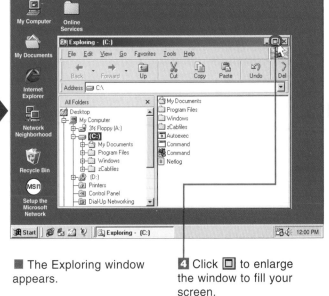

■ The Exploring window appears.

4 Click ▢ to enlarge the window to fill your screen.

How can I work with files in Windows Explorer?

You can work with files in Windows Explorer as you would work with files in a My Computer window. For example, you can move, rename and delete files in Windows Explorer.

Windows Explorer   **My Computer**

Note: For more information on working with files, see pages 76 to 103.

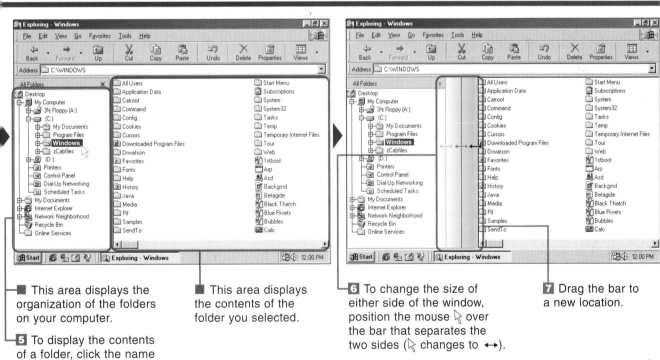

■ This area displays the organization of the folders on your computer.

5 To display the contents of a folder, click the name of the folder.

■ This area displays the contents of the folder you selected.

6 To change the size of either side of the window, position the mouse ⬧ over the bar that separates the two sides (⬧ changes to ↔).

7 Drag the bar to a new location.

CONTINUED

USING WINDOWS EXPLORER

A folder may contain other folders. You can easily display or hide these folders at any time.

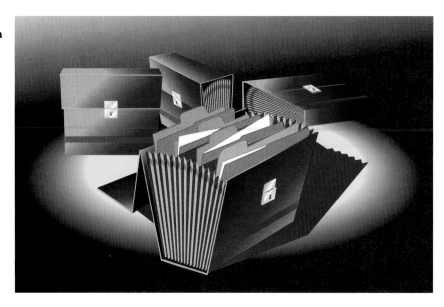

DISPLAY HIDDEN FOLDERS

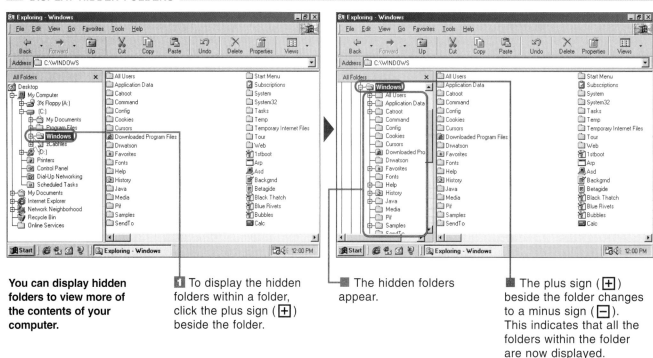

You can display hidden folders to view more of the contents of your computer.

■1 To display the hidden folders within a folder, click the plus sign (⊞) beside the folder.

■ The hidden folders appear.

■ The plus sign (⊞) beside the folder changes to a minus sign (⊟). This indicates that all the folders within the folder are now displayed.

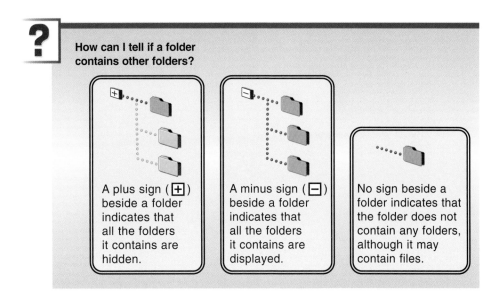

How can I tell if a folder contains other folders?

A plus sign (⊞) beside a folder indicates that all the folders it contains are hidden.

A minus sign (⊟) beside a folder indicates that all the folders it contains are displayed.

No sign beside a folder indicates that the folder does not contain any folders, although it may contain files.

◼ HIDE FOLDERS ◼

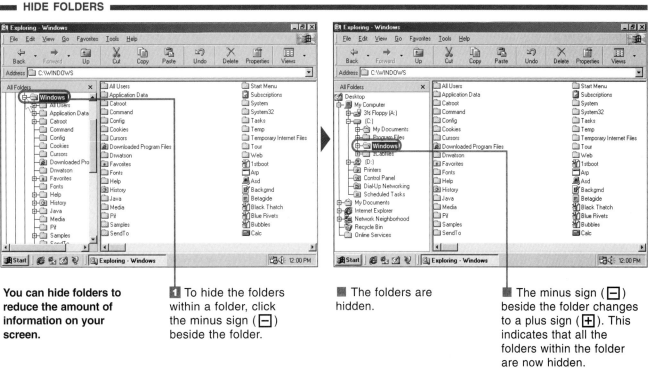

You can hide folders to reduce the amount of information on your screen.

1 To hide the folders within a folder, click the minus sign (⊟) beside the folder.

◼ The folders are hidden.

◼ The minus sign (⊟) beside the folder changes to a plus sign (⊞). This indicates that all the folders within the folder are now hidden.

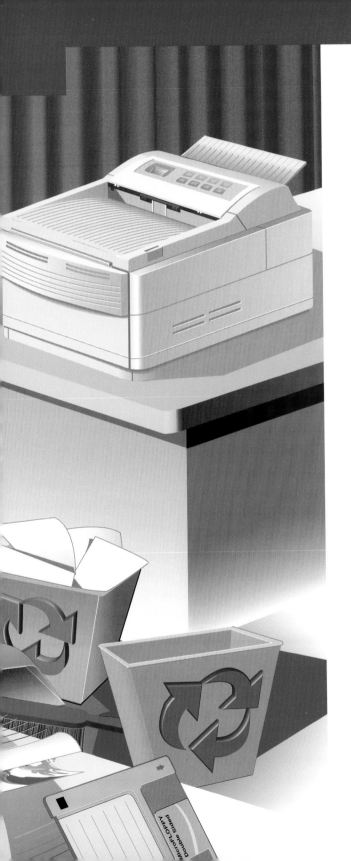

CHAPTER 5

Work with Files

There are many ways you can manage the files stored on your computer. This chapter will show you how to open, copy and print a file, plus much more.

OPEN A FILE

You can open a file to display its contents on your screen. This lets you review and make changes to the file.

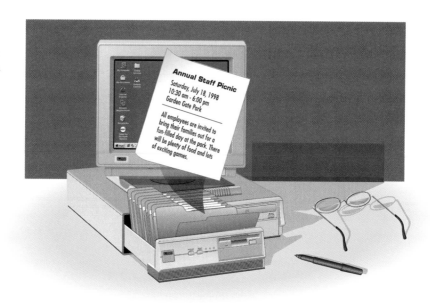

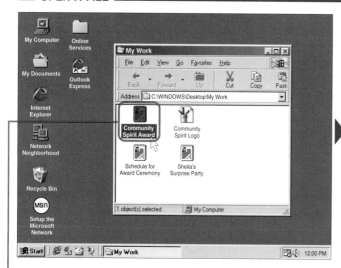

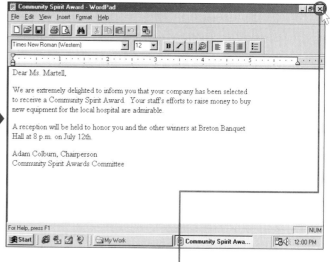

1 Double-click the file you want to open.

■ The file opens. You can review and make changes to the file.

2 When you finish working with the file, click ☒ to close the file.

OPEN A RECENTLY USED FILE

Windows remembers the files you most recently used. You can quickly open any of these files.

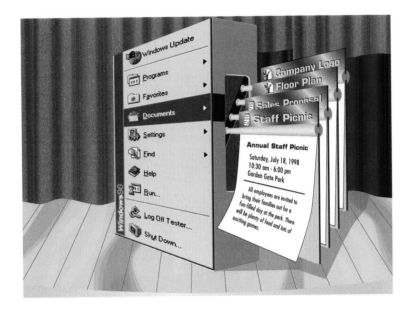

OPEN A RECENTLY USED FILE

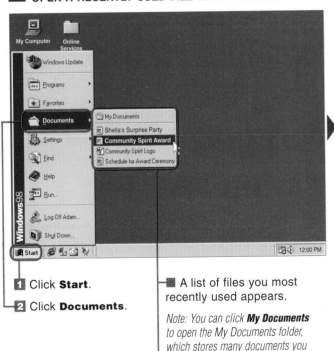

1 Click **Start**.

2 Click **Documents**.

■ A list of files you most recently used appears.

Note: You can click My Documents to open the My Documents folder, which stores many documents you have created.

3 Click the file you want to open.

■ The file opens. You can review and make changes to the file.

4 When you finish working with the file, click ✕ to close the file.

SELECT FILES

Before working with files, you must first select the files you want to work with. Selected files appear highlighted on your screen.

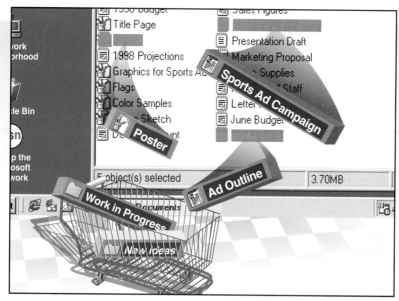

You can select folders the same way you select files. Selecting a folder will select all the files in the folder.

SELECT FILES

SELECT ONE FILE

1 Click the file you want to select.

■ The file is highlighted.

■ This area displays the number of files you selected.

? How do I deselect files?

To deselect all of the files in a window, click a blank area in the window.

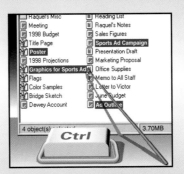

To deselect one file from a group of selected files, press and hold down the **Ctrl** key while you click the file you want to deselect.

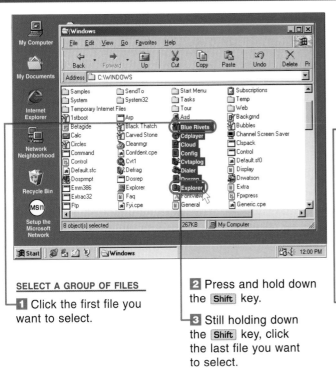

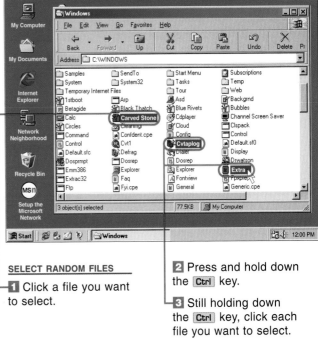

SELECT A GROUP OF FILES

1 Click the first file you want to select.

2 Press and hold down the **Shift** key.

3 Still holding down the **Shift** key, click the last file you want to select.

SELECT RANDOM FILES

1 Click a file you want to select.

2 Press and hold down the **Ctrl** key.

3 Still holding down the **Ctrl** key, click each file you want to select.

RENAME A FILE

You can give a file a new name to better describe the contents of the file. This can make the file easier to find.

RENAME A FILE

1 Click the file you want to rename.

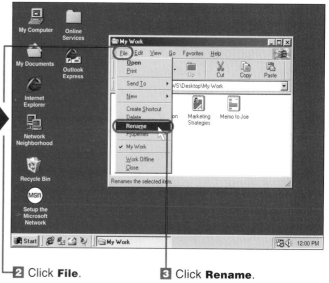

2 Click **File**.

3 Click **Rename**.

Can I rename a folder?

You should only rename folders that you have created. To rename a folder, perform the steps below, selecting the folder you want to rename in step **1**.

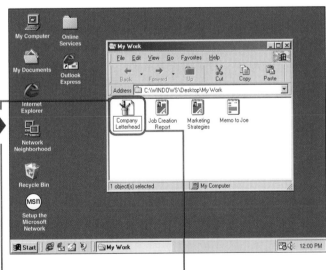

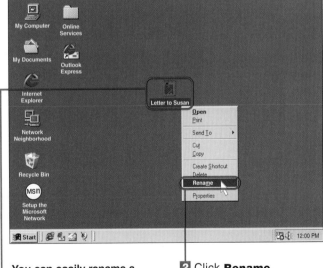

■ The name of the file appears in a box.

4 Type a new name for the file and then press the Enter key.

Note: You can use up to 255 characters to name a file. The name cannot contain the \ /:*?"< > or | characters.

You can easily rename a file on your desktop.

1 Click the file using the **right** mouse button. A menu appears.

2 Click **Rename**.

3 Type a new name and then press the Enter key.

CREATE A NEW FOLDER

You can create a new folder to help you better organize the information stored on your computer. Creating a folder is like placing a new folder in a filing cabinet.

CREATE A NEW FOLDER

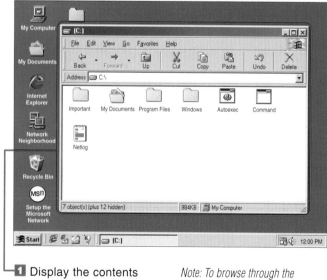

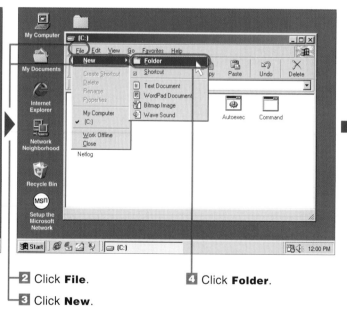

1 Display the contents of the folder where you want to place the new folder.

Note: To browse through the contents of your computer, see page 62.

2 Click **File**.

3 Click **New**.

4 Click **Folder**.

How can creating new folders help me organize the information on my computer?

You can create as many new folders as you need to develop a filing system that works for you. You can then organize your files by moving them to the new folders. To move files, see page 84.

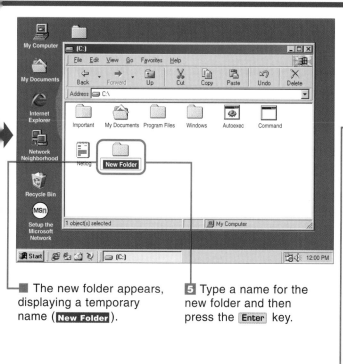

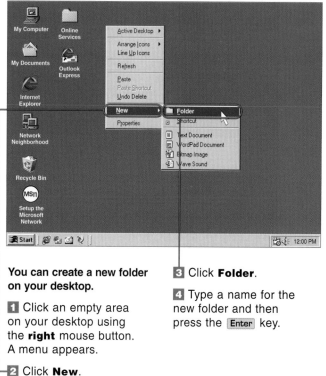

■ The new folder appears, displaying a temporary name (**New Folder**).

5 Type a name for the new folder and then press the **Enter** key.

You can create a new folder on your desktop.

1 Click an empty area on your desktop using the **right** mouse button. A menu appears.

2 Click **New**.

3 Click **Folder**.

4 Type a name for the new folder and then press the **Enter** key.

MOVE AND COPY FILES

You can organize the files
stored on your computer
by moving or copying
them to new locations.

Organizing files on
your computer is
similar to organizing
files in a filing cabinet.

MOVE FILES

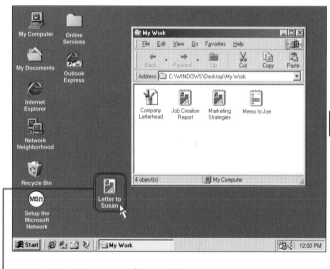

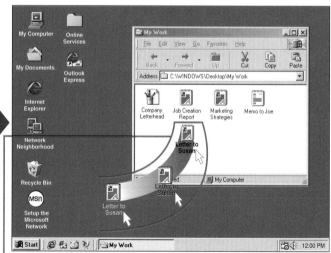

1 Position the mouse ⬉
over the file you want
to move.

■ To move more than one
file, select all the files you
want to move. Then position
the mouse ⬉ over one of
the files.

*Note: To select multiple files,
see page 79.*

2 Drag the file to a new
location on your computer.

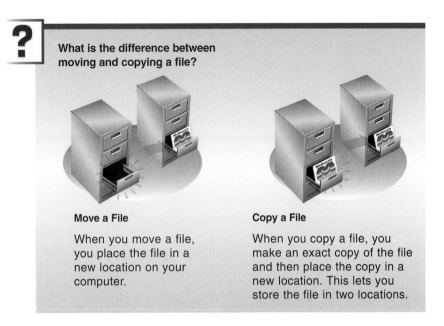

What is the difference between moving and copying a file?

Move a File

When you move a file, you place the file in a new location on your computer.

Copy a File

When you copy a file, you make an exact copy of the file and then place the copy in a new location. This lets you store the file in two locations.

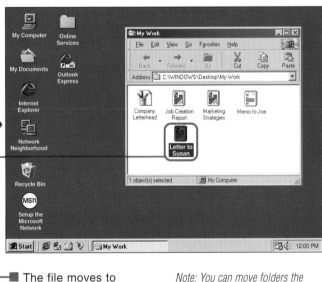

■ The file moves to the new location.

Note: You can move folders the same way you move files. When you move a folder, all the files in the folder also move.

COPY FILES

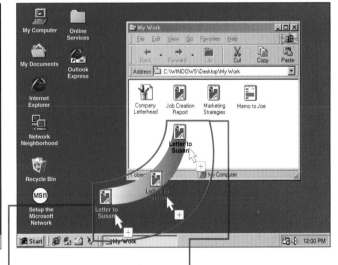

1 Position the mouse over the file you want to copy.

2 Press and hold down the `Ctrl` key.

3 Still holding down the `Ctrl` key, drag the file to a new location.

COPY A FILE TO A FLOPPY DISK

You can make an exact copy of a file and then place the copy on a floppy disk. This is useful if you want to give a colleague a copy of the file.

COPY A FILE TO A FLOPPY DISK

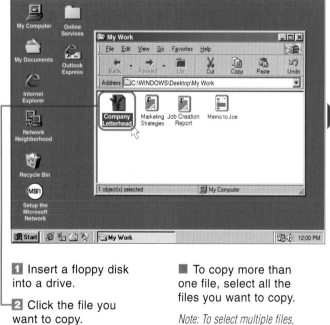

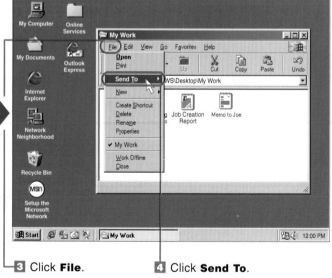

1 Insert a floppy disk into a drive.

2 Click the file you want to copy.

■ To copy more than one file, select all the files you want to copy.

Note: To select multiple files, see page 79.

3 Click **File**.

4 Click **Send To**.

?

How can I protect the information on my floppy disks?

You should keep floppy disks away from magnets, which can damage the information stored on the disks. Also be careful not to spill liquids, such as coffee or soda, on the disks.

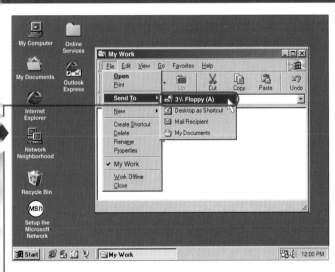

5 Click the drive that contains the floppy disk you want to receive a copy of the file.

■ Windows places a copy of the file on the floppy disk.

Note: You can copy a folder the same way you copy a file. When you copy a folder, all the files in the folder are also copied.

You can copy a file from your desktop to a floppy disk.

1 Insert a floppy disk into a drive.

2 Click the file you want to copy using the **right** mouse button. A menu appears.

3 Click **Send To**.

4 Click the drive that contains the floppy disk you want to receive a copy of the file.

DELETE A FILE

You can delete a file you no longer need.

Before you delete any files you have created, consider the value of your work. Do not delete a file unless you are certain you no longer need the file.

■ DELETE A FILE ■

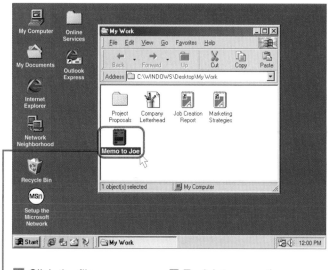

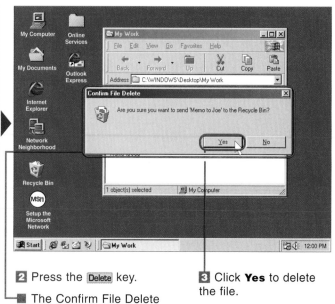

1 Click the file you want to delete.

■ To delete more than one file, select the files.

Note: To select multiple files, see page 79.

2 Press the Delete key.

■ The Confirm File Delete dialog box appears.

3 Click **Yes** to delete the file.

Can I delete any file on my computer?

Make sure you only delete files that you have created. Do not delete any files that Windows or other programs require to operate.

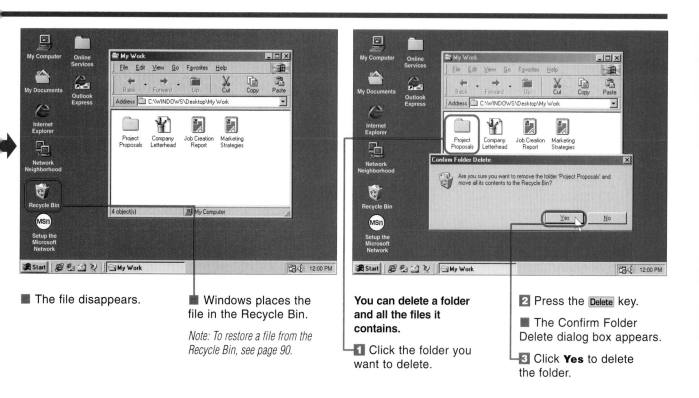

■ The file disappears.

■ Windows places the file in the Recycle Bin.

Note: To restore a file from the Recycle Bin, see page 90.

You can delete a folder and all the files it contains.

◆1 Click the folder you want to delete.

◆2 Press the Delete key.

■ The Confirm Folder Delete dialog box appears.

◆3 Click **Yes** to delete the folder.

RESTORE A DELETED FILE

The Recycle Bin stores all the files you have deleted. You can easily restore any of these files.

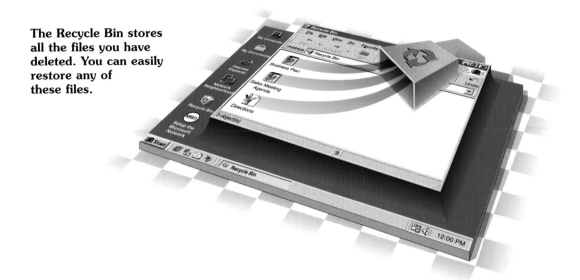

RESTORE A DELETED FILE

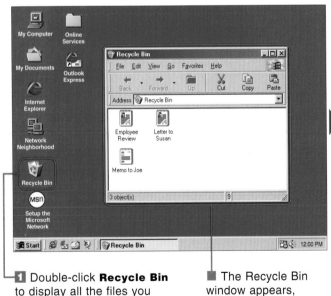

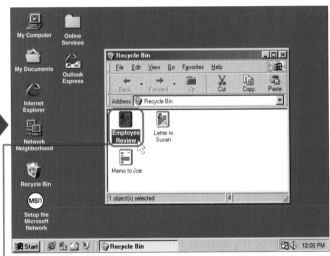

1 Double-click **Recycle Bin** to display all the files you have deleted.

■ The Recycle Bin window appears, displaying all the files you have deleted.

2 Click the file you want to restore.

■ To restore more than one file, select the files.

Note: To select multiple files, see page 79.

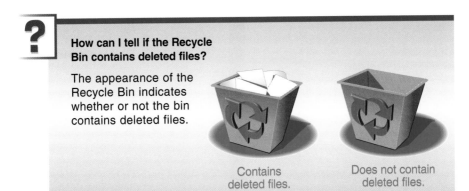

How can I tell if the Recycle Bin contains deleted files?

The appearance of the Recycle Bin indicates whether or not the bin contains deleted files.

Contains deleted files.

Does not contain deleted files.

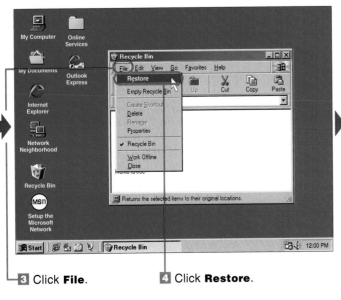

3 Click **File**.

4 Click **Restore**.

■ The file disappears from the Recycle Bin window. Windows places the file back in its original location.

5 Click ☒ to close the Recycle Bin window.

Note: You can restore folders the same way you restore files. When you restore a folder, all the files in the folder are also restored.

EMPTY THE RECYCLE BIN

You can create more free space on your computer by permanently removing all the files from the Recycle Bin.

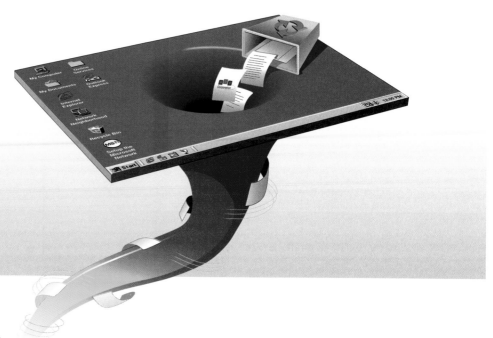

EMPTY THE RECYCLE BIN

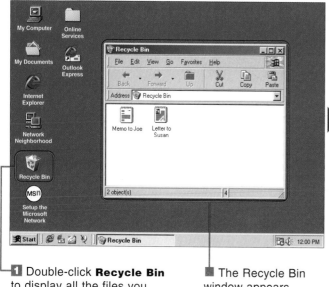

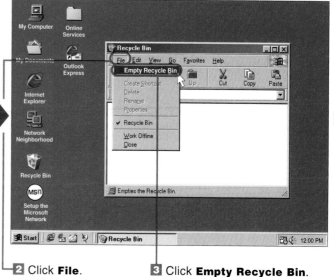

1 Double-click **Recycle Bin** to display all the files you have deleted.

■ The Recycle Bin window appears, displaying all the files you have deleted.

2 Click **File**.

3 Click **Empty Recycle Bin**.

What if the Recycle Bin contains a file I may need?

Before emptying the Recycle Bin, make sure it does not contain files you may need in the future. To restore a file you may need, see page 90. Once you empty the Recycle Bin, the files are permanently removed from your computer and cannot be restored.

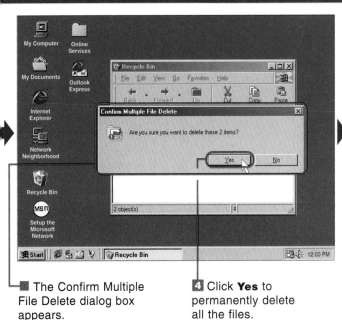

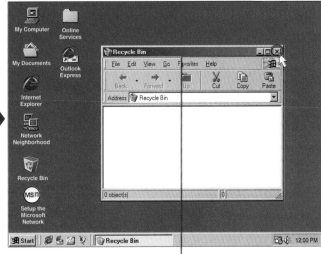

■ The Confirm Multiple File Delete dialog box appears.

4 Click **Yes** to permanently delete all the files.

■ All the files are permanently deleted from your computer.

5 Click ☒ to close the Recycle Bin window.

PRINT A FILE

You can produce a paper copy of a file stored on your computer. Before printing, make sure your printer is turned on and contains paper.

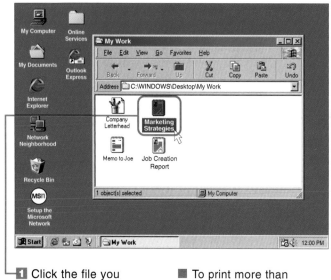

1 Click the file you want to print.

■ To print more than one file, select the files.

Note: To select multiple files, see page 79.

2 Click **File**.

3 Click **Print**.

What types of printers can I use to print my files?

Windows works with many types of printers. There are two common types of printers.

Ink-jet

An ink-jet printer produces documents that are suitable for routine business and personal use.

Laser

A laser printer is faster and produces higher-quality documents than an ink-jet printer, but is more expensive.

■ When you print a file, the printer icon (🖨) appears in this area. The icon disappears when the file has finished printing.

You can print a file located on your desktop.

◄1 Click the file you want to print using the **right** mouse button. A menu appears.

2 Click **Print**.

VIEW FILES SENT TO THE PRINTER

You can view information about the files you sent to the printer.

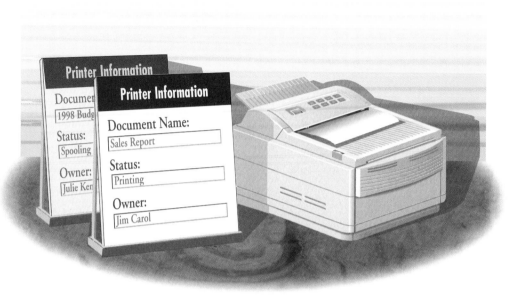

VIEW FILES SENT TO THE PRINTER

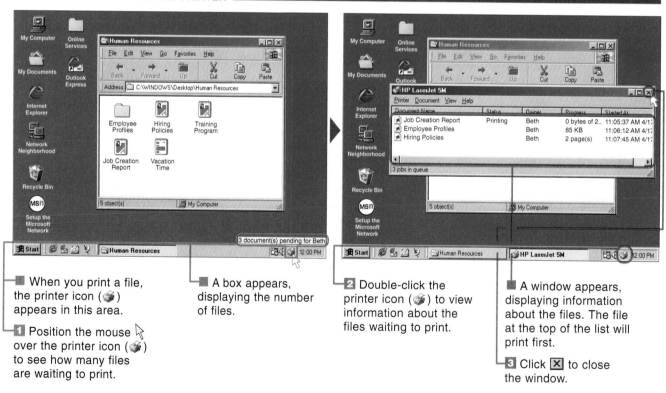

■ When you print a file, the printer icon (🖨) appears in this area.

1 Position the mouse over the printer icon (🖨) to see how many files are waiting to print.

■ A box appears, displaying the number of files.

2 Double-click the printer icon (🖨) to view information about the files waiting to print.

■ A window appears, displaying information about the files. The file at the top of the list will print first.

3 Click ☒ to close the window.

You can stop a file
from printing. This is
useful if you want to
make last-minute
changes to the file.

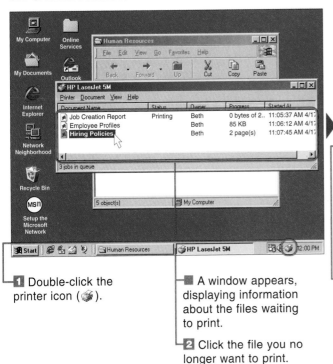

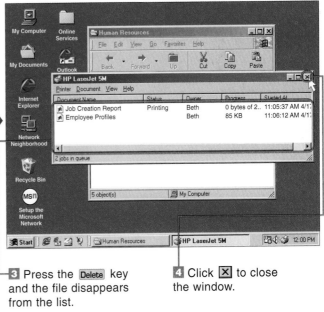

1 Double-click the
printer icon (🖨).

■ A window appears,
displaying information
about the files waiting
to print.

2 Click the file you no
longer want to print.

3 Press the Delete key
and the file disappears
from the list.

4 Click ☒ to close
the window.

FIND A FILE

If you cannot remember the exact name or location of a file you want to work with, you can have Windows search for the file.

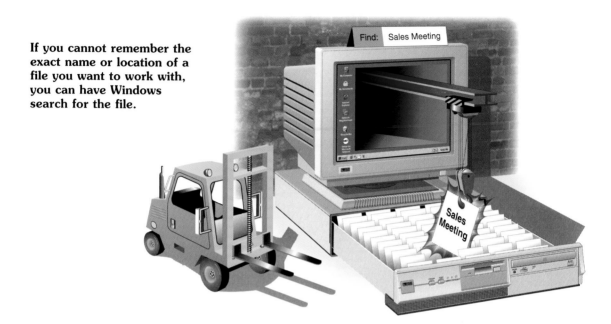

Find: Sales Meeting

FIND A FILE

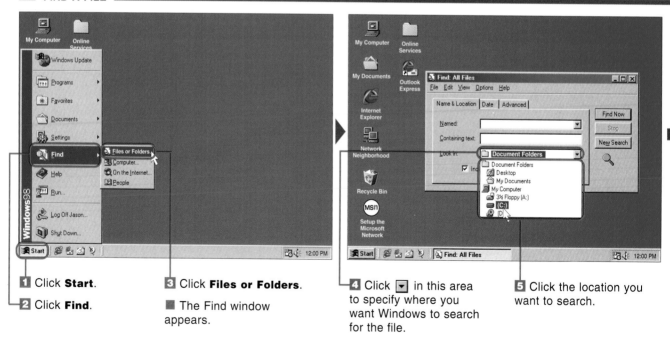

1 Click **Start**.

2 Click **Find**.

3 Click **Files or Folders**.

■ The Find window appears.

4 Click ▾ in this area to specify where you want Windows to search for the file.

5 Click the location you want to search.

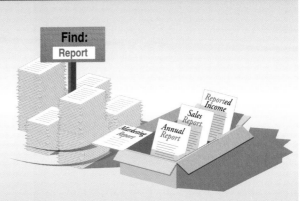

Can I search for a file if I only know part of the file name?

If you search for part of a file name, Windows will find all the files and folders with names that contain the word you specified. For example, searching for the word "report" will find every file or folder with a name containing the word "report".

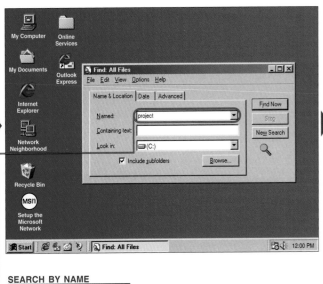

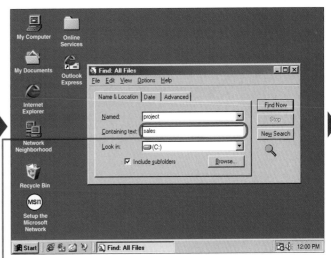

SEARCH BY NAME

6 To specify the name of the file you want to find, click this area. Then type all or part of the name.

SEARCH BY CONTENT

7 To specify a word or phrase within the file you want to find, click this area. Then type the word or phrase.

CONTINUED

FIND A FILE

You can search for a file you worked with during a specific time period. You can also search for a specific type of file, such as files created in WordPad.

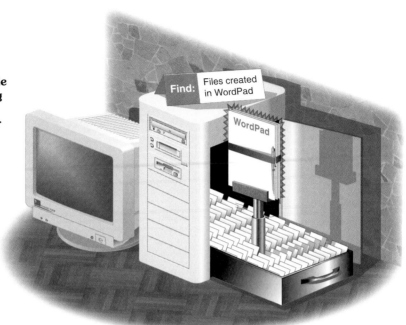

Find: Files created in WordPad

WordPad

FIND A FILE (CONTINUED)

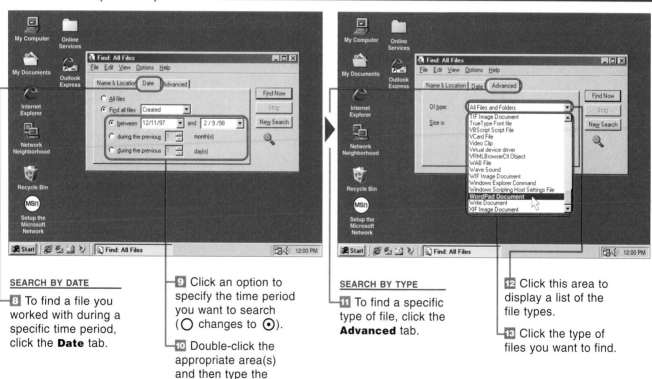

SEARCH BY DATE

8 To find a file you worked with during a specific time period, click the **Date** tab.

9 Click an option to specify the time period you want to search (○ changes to ⊙).

10 Double-click the appropriate area(s) and then type the time period.

SEARCH BY TYPE

11 To find a specific type of file, click the **Advanced** tab.

12 Click this area to display a list of the file types.

13 Click the type of files you want to find.

How can I find all the programs on my computer?

To find all the programs on your computer, perform steps 1 to 5 on page 98 and then perform steps 11 to 14, selecting **Application** in step 13.

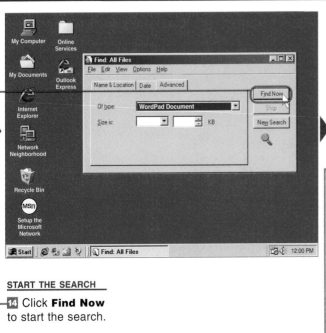

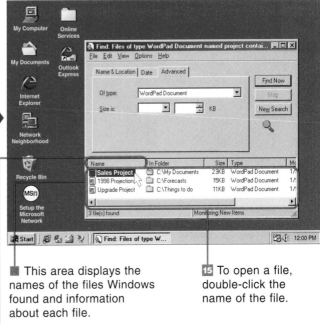

START THE SEARCH

14 Click **Find Now** to start the search.

■ This area displays the names of the files Windows found and information about each file.

■ If Windows found several files, you can click the **Name** heading to sort the files alphabetically.

15 To open a file, double-click the name of the file.

ADD A SHORTCUT TO THE DESKTOP

You can add a shortcut to
the desktop to provide a
quick way of opening a
file you use regularly.

ADD A SHORTCUT TO THE DESKTOP

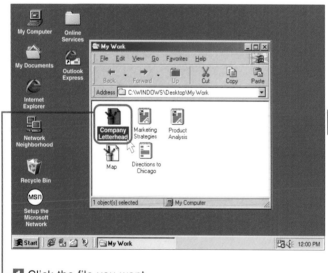

1 Click the file you want
to create a shortcut to.

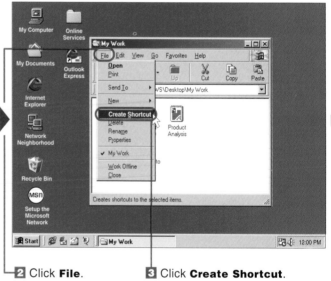

2 Click **File**.

3 Click **Create Shortcut**.

? How do I rename or delete a shortcut?

You can rename or delete a shortcut the same way you would rename or delete any file. Renaming or deleting a shortcut does not affect the original file. For information on renaming a file, see page 80. For information on deleting a file, see page 88.

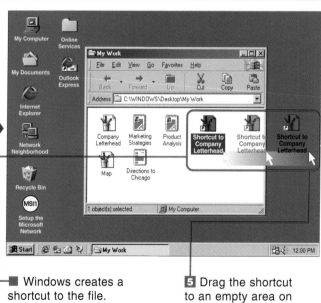

■ Windows creates a shortcut to the file.

4 Position the mouse over the shortcut.

5 Drag the shortcut to an empty area on your desktop.

■ The shortcut appears on the desktop.

■ You can tell the difference between the original file and the shortcut because the shortcut displays an arrow (🗗).

■ You can double-click the shortcut to open the file.

CHAPTER 6

Customize Windows

Windows includes a number of features that allow you to personalize your computer. In this chapter you will learn how to change Windows settings to suit your needs.

MOVE THE TASKBAR

You can move the
taskbar to a more
convenient location
on your screen.

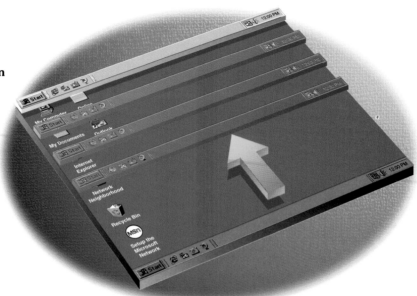

MOVE THE TASKBAR

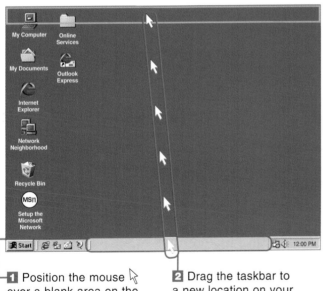

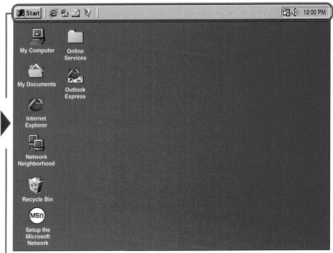

1 Position the mouse over a blank area on the taskbar.

2 Drag the taskbar to a new location on your screen.

■ The taskbar moves to the new location.

Note: You can move the taskbar to the top, bottom, left or right edge of your screen.

You can change the size
of the taskbar so it can
display more information.

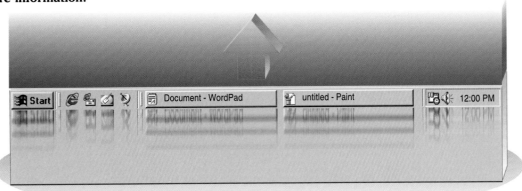

SIZE THE TASKBAR

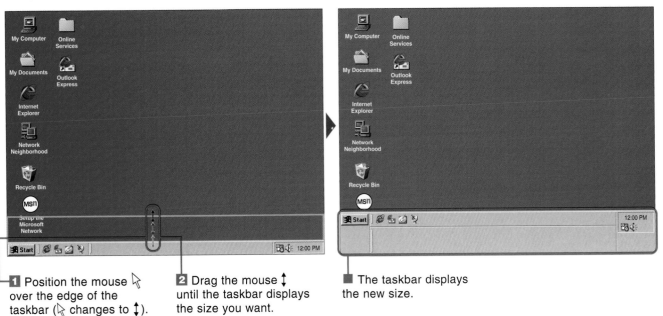

1 Position the mouse ↳
over the edge of the
taskbar (↳ changes to ↕).

2 Drag the mouse ↕
until the taskbar displays
the size you want.

■ The taskbar displays
the new size.

HIDE THE TASKBAR

You can hide the taskbar to give you more room on the screen to accomplish tasks.

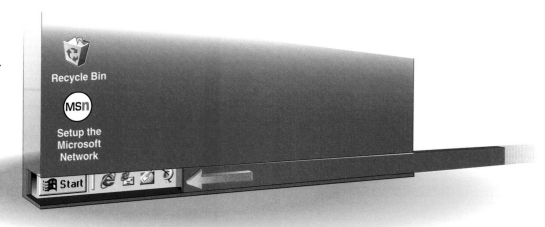

HIDE THE TASKBAR

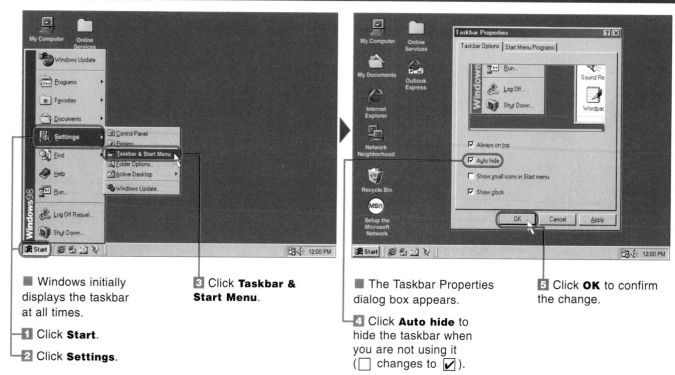

■ Windows initially displays the taskbar at all times.

◀1 Click **Start**.

◀2 Click **Settings**.

3 Click **Taskbar & Start Menu**.

■ The Taskbar Properties dialog box appears.

4 Click **Auto hide** to hide the taskbar when you are not using it (☐ changes to ☑).

5 Click **OK** to confirm the change.

?

What information does the taskbar display?

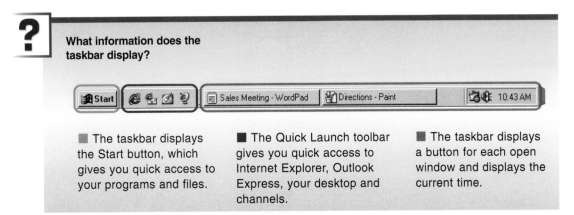

■ The taskbar displays the Start button, which gives you quick access to your programs and files.

■ The Quick Launch toolbar gives you quick access to Internet Explorer, Outlook Express, your desktop and channels.

■ The taskbar displays a button for each open window and displays the current time.

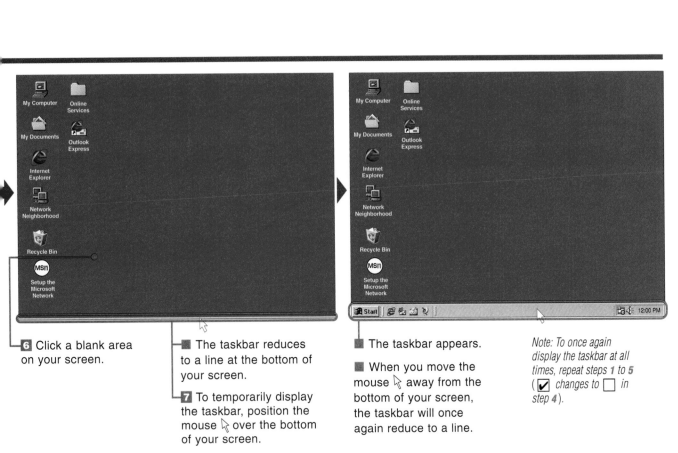

6 Click a blank area on your screen.

■ The taskbar reduces to a line at the bottom of your screen.

7 To temporarily display the taskbar, position the mouse ⬚ over the bottom of your screen.

■ The taskbar appears.

■ When you move the mouse ⬚ away from the bottom of your screen, the taskbar will once again reduce to a line.

Note: To once again display the taskbar at all times, repeat steps 1 to 5 (☑ changes to ☐ in step 4).

CHANGE THE DATE AND TIME

You should make sure the correct date and time are set in your computer. Windows uses this information to determine when you create and update your documents.

CHANGE THE DATE AND TIME

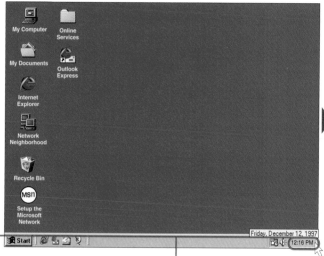

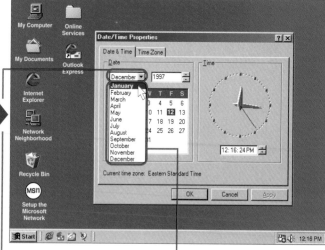

■ This area displays the time set in your computer.

1 To display the date set in your computer, position the mouse ▷ over this area. A box appears, displaying the date.

2 To change the date or time set in your computer, double-click this area.

■ The Date/Time Properties dialog box appears.

■ This area displays the month set in your computer.

3 To change the month, click this area.

4 Click the correct month.

Will Windows keep track of the date and time even when I turn off my computer?

Your computer has a built-in clock that keeps track of the date and time even when you turn off the computer.

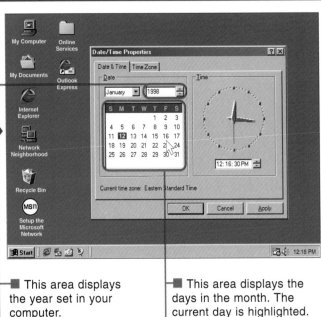

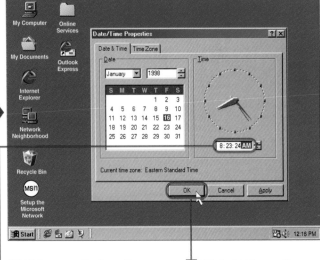

■ This area displays the year set in your computer.

5 To change the year, click ▲ or ▼ in this area until the correct year appears.

■ This area displays the days in the month. The current day is highlighted.

6 To change the day, click the correct day.

■ This area displays the time set in your computer.

7 To change the time, double-click the part of the time you want to change. Then type the correct information.

8 Click **OK** to confirm your changes.

ADD WALLPAPER

You can decorate
your screen by
adding wallpaper.

■■ **ADD WALLPAPER** ■■■■■■■■■■■■■■■

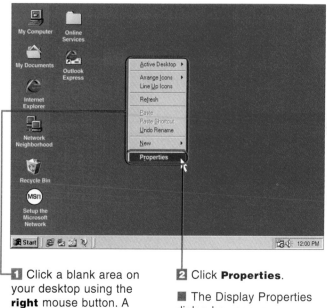

1 Click a blank area on
your desktop using the
right mouse button. A
menu appears.

2 Click **Properties**.

■ The Display Properties
dialog box appears.

3 Click the wallpaper
you want to use.

4 Click this area to
select how you want to
display the wallpaper
on your screen.

5 Click the way you
want to display the
wallpaper.

*Note: For more information,
see the top of page 113.*

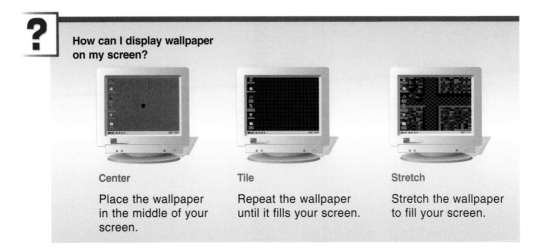

How can I display wallpaper on my screen?

Center

Place the wallpaper in the middle of your screen.

Tile

Repeat the wallpaper until it fills your screen.

Stretch

Stretch the wallpaper to fill your screen.

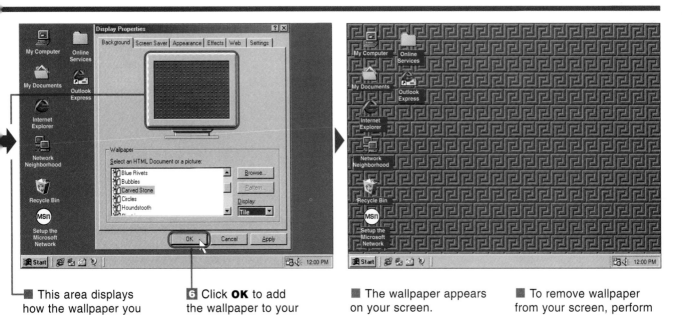

■ This area displays how the wallpaper you selected will look on your screen.

6 Click **OK** to add the wallpaper to your screen.

■ The wallpaper appears on your screen.

■ To remove wallpaper from your screen, perform steps **1** to **3**, selecting **(None)** in step **3**. Then perform step **6**.

SET UP A SCREEN SAVER

A screen saver is a moving
picture or pattern that
appears on the screen
when you do not use
your computer for a
period of time.

SET UP A SCREEN SAVER

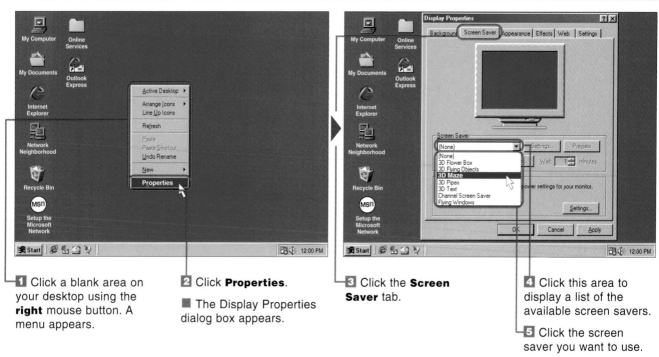

1 Click a blank area on
your desktop using the
right mouse button. A
menu appears.

2 Click **Properties**.

■ The Display Properties
dialog box appears.

3 Click the **Screen
Saver** tab.

4 Click this area to
display a list of the
available screen savers.

5 Click the screen
saver you want to use.

?

Do I need to use a screen saver?

Screen savers were originally designed to prevent screen burn, which occurs when an image appears in a fixed position on the screen for a period of time. Today's monitors are better designed to prevent screen burn, but people still use screen savers for their entertainment value.

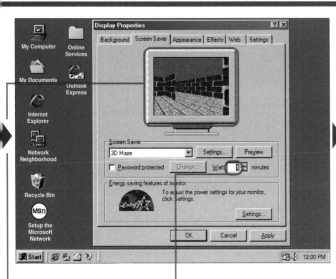

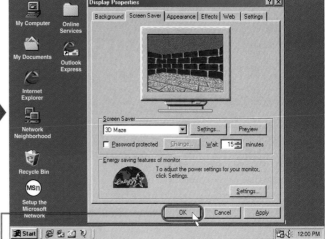

■ This area displays how the screen saver will look on your screen.

■ The screen saver will appear when you do not use your computer for the number of minutes shown in this area.

6 To change the number of minutes, double-click this area. Then type a new number.

7 Click **OK** to turn the screen saver on.

■ When the screen saver appears on your screen, you can move the mouse or press a key on your keyboard to remove the screen saver.

■ To turn the screen saver off, perform steps **1** to **5**, selecting **(None)** in step **5**. Then perform step **7**.

CHANGE SCREEN COLORS

You can change the colors displayed on your screen to personalize and enhance Windows.

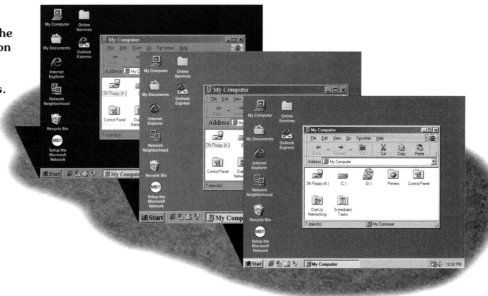

CHANGE SCREEN COLORS

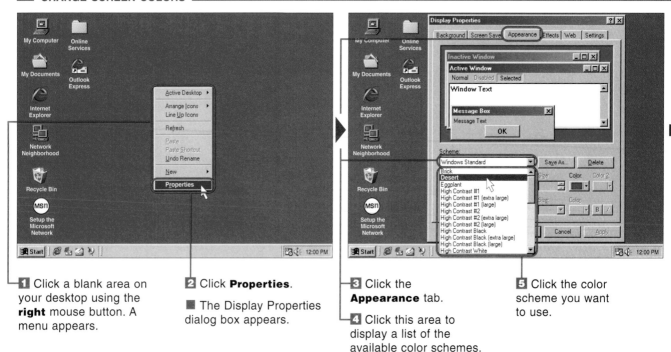

1 Click a blank area on your desktop using the **right** mouse button. A menu appears.

2 Click **Properties**.

■ The Display Properties dialog box appears.

3 Click the **Appearance** tab.

4 Click this area to display a list of the available color schemes.

5 Click the color scheme you want to use.

?

What is the difference between the High Contrast, high color and VGA color schemes?

High Contrast schemes are designed for people with vision impairments.

High color schemes are designed for computers displaying more than 256 colors.

VGA schemes are designed for computers limited to 16 colors.

Note: For information on changing the number of colors your computer displays, see page 122.

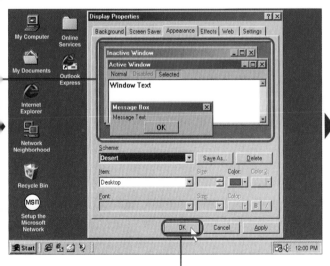

◀■ This area displays how your screen will look with the color scheme you selected.

6 Click **OK** to add the color scheme.

■ Your screen displays the color scheme you selected.

■ To return to the original color scheme, perform steps **1** to **6**, selecting **Windows Standard** in step **5**.

USING A DESKTOP THEME

You can use a desktop theme to customize the appearance of your desktop. There are several themes available, including baseball, jungle and mystery.

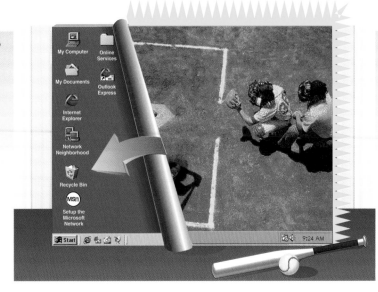

Before you can use a desktop theme, you may need to add the Desktop Themes component to your computer. To add a Windows component, see page 178.

see page 178.

■■■ **USING A DESKTOP THEME** ■■■

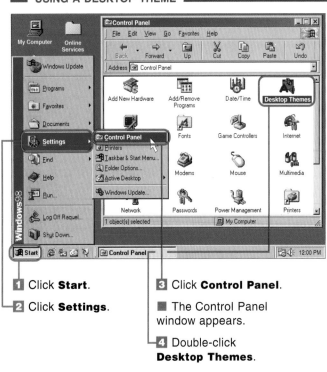

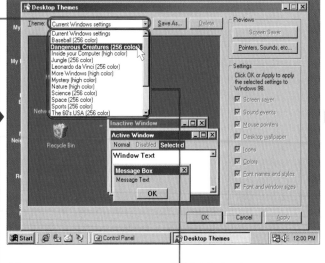

1 Click **Start**.

2 Click **Settings**.

3 Click **Control Panel**.

■ The Control Panel window appears.

4 Double-click **Desktop Themes**.

■ The Desktop Themes window appears.

5 Click this area to display a list of the available themes.

6 Click the theme you want to use.

If I add a desktop theme, what items will change?

A desktop theme will change the colors, sounds, wallpaper, screen saver, mouse pointers and icons on your computer.

■ This area displays a preview of the theme you selected.

7 Windows will apply the theme to each setting that displays a check mark (☑). You can click a setting to add or remove a check mark.

8 Click **OK** to confirm your changes.

■ The desktop theme you selected appears.

■ To return to the original desktop theme, perform steps 1 to 8, selecting **Windows Default** in step 6.

CHANGE SCREEN RESOLUTION

You can change the amount of information that can fit on your screen.

Lower resolutions display larger images on the screen. This lets you see information more clearly.

Higher resolutions display smaller images on the screen. This lets you display more information at once.

▬ CHANGE SCREEN RESOLUTION ▬

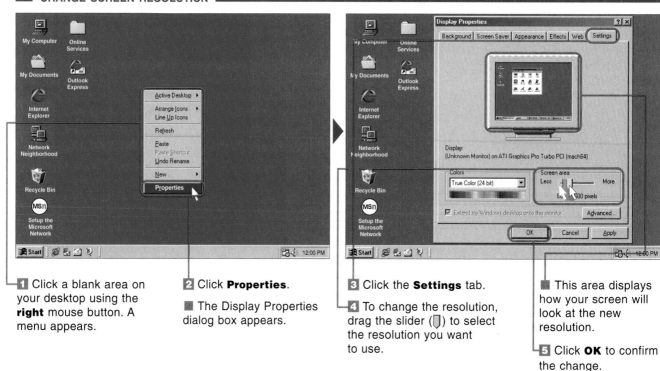

■1 Click a blank area on your desktop using the **right** mouse button. A menu appears.

■2 Click **Properties**.

■ The Display Properties dialog box appears.

■3 Click the **Settings** tab.

■4 To change the resolution, drag the slider (▯) to select the resolution you want to use.

■ This area displays how your screen will look at the new resolution.

■5 Click **OK** to confirm the change.

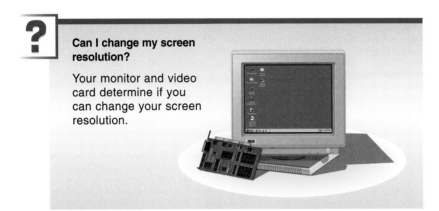

Can I change my screen resolution?

Your monitor and video card determine if you can change your screen resolution.

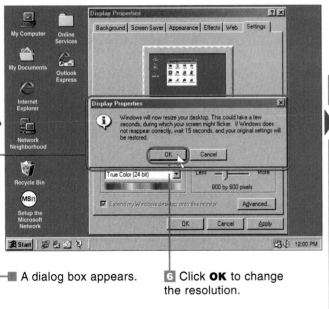

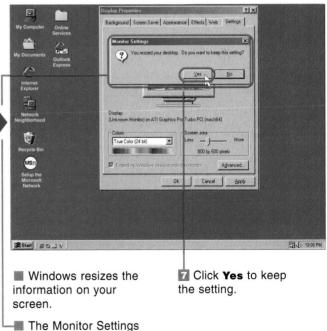

■ A dialog box appears.

6 Click **OK** to change the resolution.

■ Windows resizes the information on your screen.

■ The Monitor Settings dialog box appears, asking if you want to keep the setting.

7 Click **Yes** to keep the setting.

CHANGE COLOR DEPTH

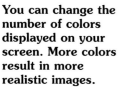

You can change the
number of colors
displayed on your
screen. More colors
result in more
realistic images.

Your monitor and
video card determine
the maximum number
of colors your screen
can display.

CHANGE COLOR DEPTH

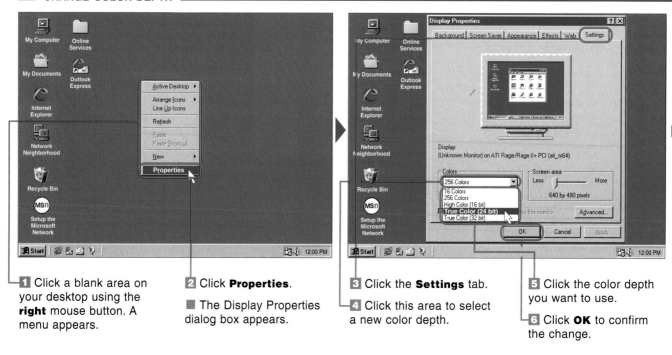

1 Click a blank area on
your desktop using the
right mouse button. A
menu appears.

2 Click **Properties**.

■ The Display Properties
dialog box appears.

3 Click the **Settings** tab.

4 Click this area to select
a new color depth.

5 Click the color depth
you want to use.

6 Click **OK** to confirm
the change.

? **When would I change the number of colors displayed on my screen?**

You may want to display more colors on your screen when viewing photographs, playing videos or playing games on your computer.

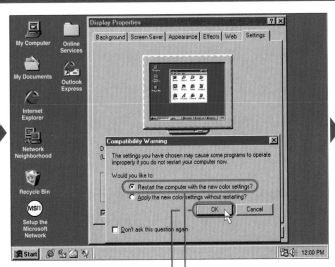

■ A dialog box appears, stating that some programs may not operate properly if you do not restart your computer.

7 Click this option to restart your computer with the new color settings (○ changes to ⊙).

8 Click **OK** to restart your computer.

■ A dialog box appears, stating that you must restart your computer before the new settings will take effect.

9 Click **Yes** to restart your computer.

CHANGE MOUSE SETTINGS

You can change the
way your mouse works
to suit your needs.

CHANGE MOUSE SETTINGS

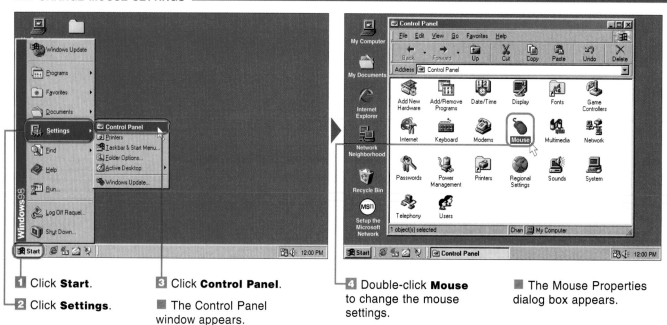

1 Click **Start**.

2 Click **Settings**.

3 Click **Control Panel**.

■ The Control Panel
window appears.

4 Double-click **Mouse**
to change the mouse
settings.

■ The Mouse Properties
dialog box appears.

Should I use a mouse pad?

A mouse pad provides a smooth surface for moving the mouse on your desk. A mouse pad reduces the amount of dirt that enters the mouse and protects your desk from scratches. Hard plastic mouse pads attract less dirt and provide a smoother surface than fabric mouse pads.

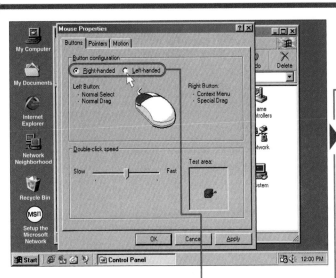

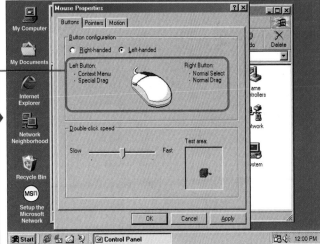

SWITCH BUTTONS

If you are left-handed, you can switch the functions of the left and right mouse buttons to make the mouse easier to use.

1 Click an option to specify if you are right-handed or left-handed (○ changes to ⊙).

■ This area describes the functions of the left and right mouse buttons, depending on the option you selected.

CONTINUED

CHANGE MOUSE SETTINGS

You can personalize your mouse by changing the double-click speed and the way the mouse pointer moves on your screen.

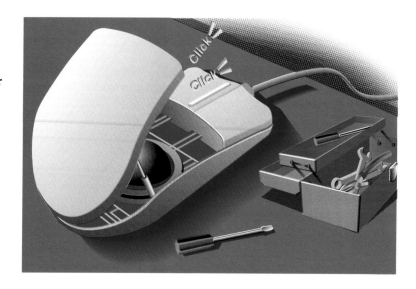

CHANGE MOUSE SETTINGS (CONTINUED)

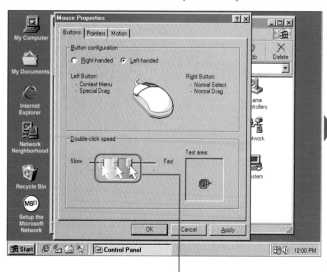

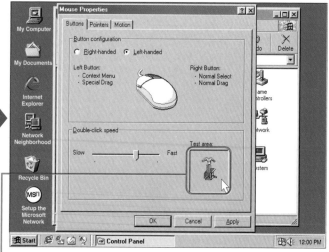

DOUBLE-CLICK SPEED

You can change the amount of time that can pass between two clicks of the mouse button for Windows to recognize a double-click.

1 Drag the slider (⬚) to a new position to change the double-click speed.

2 Double-click this area to test the double-click speed.

■ The jack-in-the-box appears if you clicked at the correct speed.

Note: If you are an inexperienced mouse user, you may find a slower speed easier to use.

Should I display pointer trails?

Displaying pointer trails can help you follow the movement of the mouse on your screen. This is especially useful on portable computer screens, where the mouse can be difficult to follow.

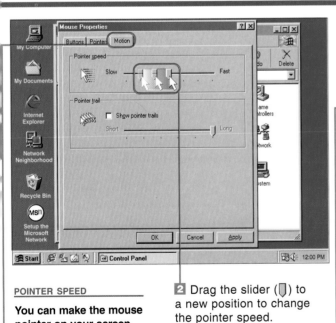

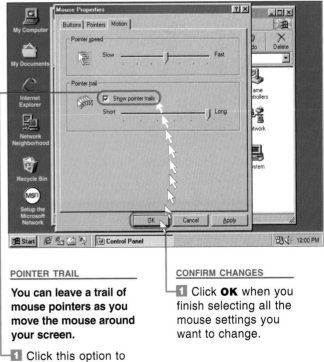

POINTER SPEED

You can make the mouse pointer on your screen move faster or slower.

1 Click the **Motion** tab.

2 Drag the slider (⬛) to a new position to change the pointer speed.

POINTER TRAIL

You can leave a trail of mouse pointers as you move the mouse around your screen.

1 Click this option to leave a trail of pointers (☐ changes to ☑).

CONFIRM CHANGES

1 Click **OK** when you finish selecting all the mouse settings you want to change.

CHANGE THE WAY YOUR COMPUTER BEHAVES

You can change the way items on your screen look and act. You can choose the Web style or the Classic style.

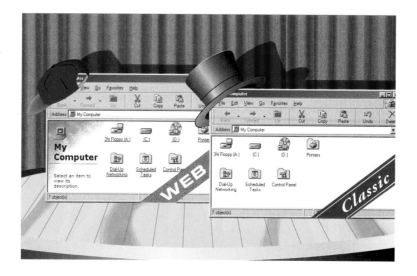

CHOOSE THE WEB OR CLASSIC STYLE

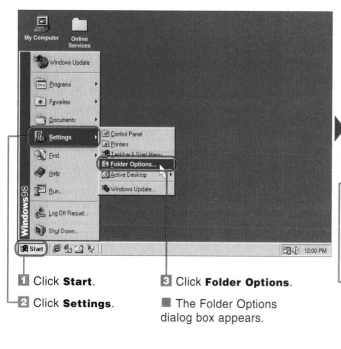

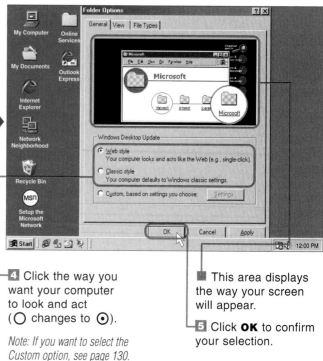

1 Click **Start**.

2 Click **Settings**.

3 Click **Folder Options**.

■ The Folder Options dialog box appears.

4 Click the way you want your computer to look and act (○ changes to ⊙).

Note: If you want to select the Custom option, see page 130.

■ This area displays the way your screen will appear.

5 Click **OK** to confirm your selection.

? **What is the difference between the Web and Classic styles?**

Web style

In the Web style, the items on your screen look and act like items on a Web page. You click items to open them. You move the mouse 🖑 over items to select them.

Classic style

In the Classic style, the items on your screen look and act the same way they did in previous versions of Windows. You double-click items to open them. You click items to select them.

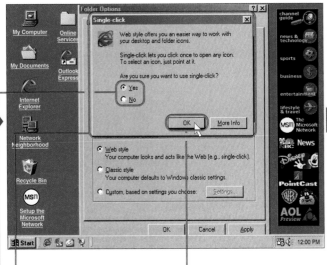

■ A dialog box appears the first time you select the Web style.

6 Click an option to specify if you want to open items using a single-click (○ changes to ⊙).

7 Click **OK** to confirm your selection.

■ When you select the Web style, your computer looks and acts like a Web page.

■ The Channel Bar may appear on your screen. For information on the Channel Bar, see page 9.

■ You can move the mouse 🖑 over an item to select the item.

■ This area displays a description of the selected item.

CONTINUED ▶

CHANGE THE WAY YOUR COMPUTER BEHAVES

You can mix and match your favorite settings to customize the way items on your screen look and act.

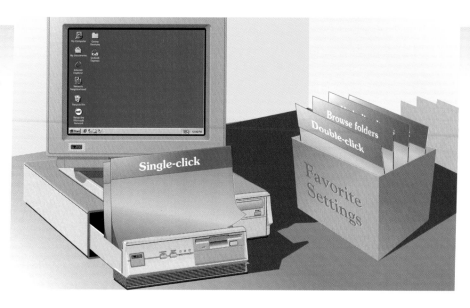

CHOOSE A CUSTOM STYLE

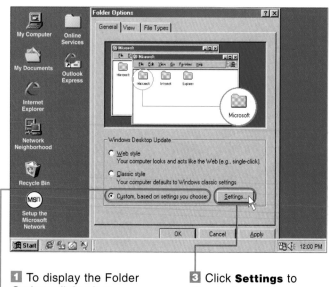

1 To display the Folder Options dialog box, perform steps **1** to **3** on page 128.

2 Click **Custom** if you want to choose your own settings.

3 Click **Settings** to choose the settings you want to use.

■ The Custom Settings dialog box appears.

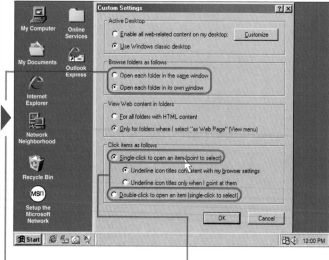

4 Click an option to open each folder in the same window or in its own window (○ changes to ⊙).

5 Click an option to open items using a single-click or a double-click (○ changes to ⊙).

Browse folders

You can choose to open each folder in the same window or in its own window.

Click items

You can choose to open items using a single-click or a double-click.

Single-click
Click the left mouse button once.

Double-click
Click the left mouse button twice.

Icon titles

If you choose to open items using a single-click, you can also choose to always underline icon titles or underline icon titles only when you move the mouse over the title.

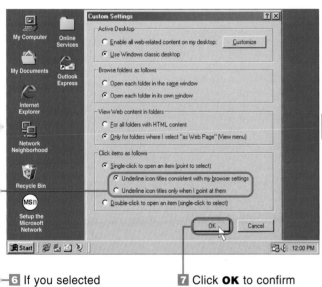

■6 If you selected Single-click in step 5, click an option to always underline icon titles or underline icon titles only when you move the mouse ☝ over the title (○ changes to ⊙).

■7 Click **OK** to confirm your changes.

■ This area displays the way your screen will appear.

■8 Click **Close** to close the dialog box.

CHANGE FOLDER APPEARANCE

You can customize the appearance of a folder by adding a background picture.

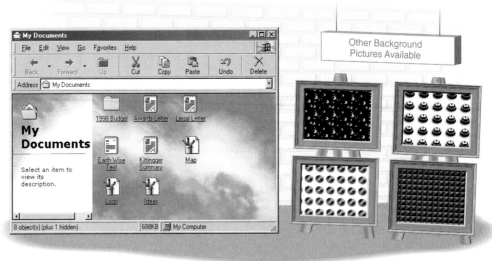

Other Background Pictures Available

CHANGE FOLDER APPEARANCE

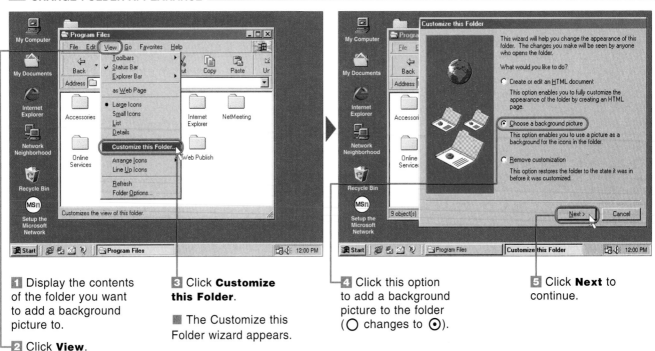

1 Display the contents of the folder you want to add a background picture to.

2 Click **View**.

3 Click **Customize this Folder**.

■ The Customize this Folder wizard appears.

4 Click this option to add a background picture to the folder (○ changes to ⊙).

5 Click **Next** to continue.

? **Why didn't the background picture appear in the folder?**

When using the Classic style, you will not see the background picture you added to a folder. To change to the Web style so you can view the background picture, see page 128.

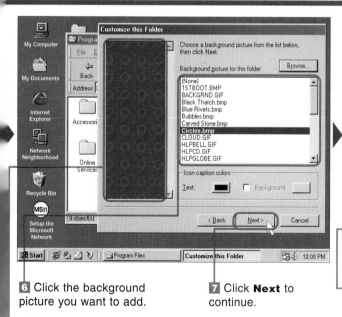

6 Click the background picture you want to add.

■ This area displays a sample of the picture you selected.

7 Click **Next** to continue.

8 Click **Finish** to change the appearance of the folder.

■ Windows adds the background picture to the folder.

■ To remove the background picture from a folder, perform steps **1** to **5**, selecting **Remove customization** in step **4**. Then perform steps **7** and **8**.

START A PROGRAM AUTOMATICALLY

If you use the same program
every day, you can have the
program start automatically
every time you turn your
computer on.

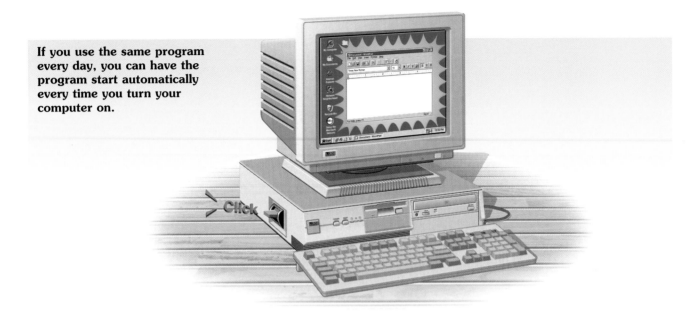

START A PROGRAM AUTOMATICALLY

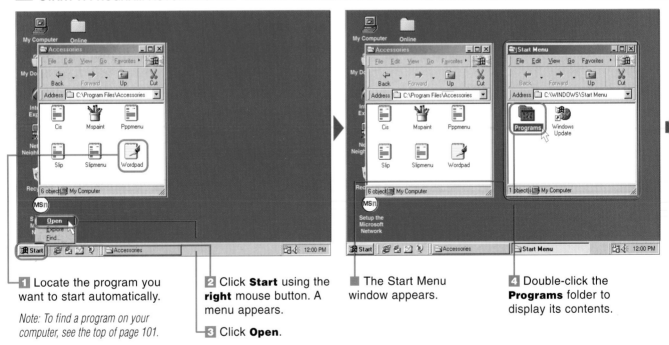

1 Locate the program you
want to start automatically.

*Note: To find a program on your
computer, see the top of page 101.*

2 Click **Start** using the
right mouse button. A
menu appears.

3 Click **Open**.

■ The Start Menu
window appears.

4 Double-click the
Programs folder to
display its contents.

How do I stop a program from starting automatically?

If you no longer want a program to start automatically, delete the shortcut for the program from the StartUp folder. You can delete a shortcut the same way you would delete a file. For information on deleting a file, see page 88. Deleting a shortcut from the StartUp folder will not remove the program from your computer.

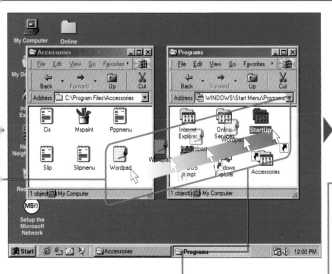

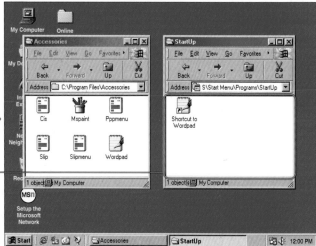

■ The contents of the Programs folder appear.

5 Position the mouse ♾ over the program you want to start automatically.

6 Drag the program to the StartUp folder.

7 Double-click the StartUp folder to display its contents.

■ The contents of the StartUp folder appear.

■ Windows placed a shortcut to the program in the folder.

Note: For information on shortcuts, see page 102.

■ The programs in the StartUp folder start automatically every time you turn your computer on.

ADD A PROGRAM TO THE START MENU

You can add your favorite programs to the Start menu so you can quickly open them.

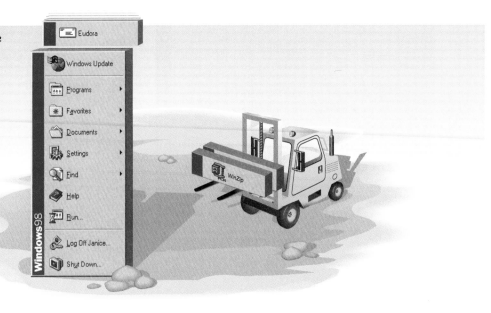

ADD A PROGRAM TO THE START MENU

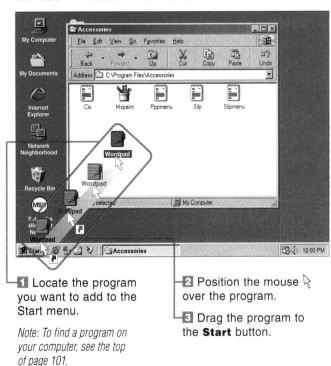

1 Locate the program you want to add to the Start menu.

Note: To find a program on your computer, see the top of page 101.

2 Position the mouse ⌖ over the program.

3 Drag the program to the **Start** button.

4 Click **Start** to display the Start menu. The Start menu appears.

■ The Start menu displays the program. You can click the program to start the program.

■ To close the Start menu without selecting an item, click outside the menu area or press the `Alt` key.

Can I add files and folders to the Start menu?

You can perform the steps on page 136 to add a file or folder to the Start menu. Adding files and folders you frequently use to the Start menu saves you the time of searching for them on your computer.

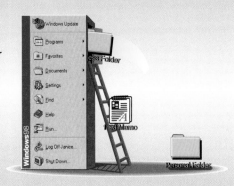

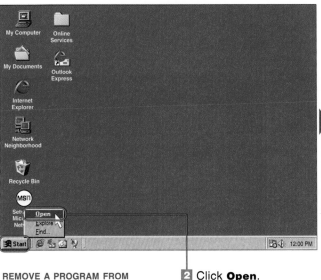

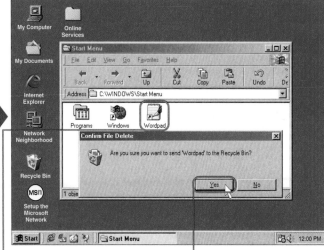

REMOVE A PROGRAM FROM THE START MENU

1 Click **Start** using the **right** mouse button. A menu appears.

2 Click **Open**.

■ The Start Menu window appears.

3 Click the program you no longer want to appear on the Start menu.

4 Press the Delete key.

■ A confirmation dialog box appears.

5 Click **Yes** to remove the program from the Start menu.

Note: Removing a program from the Start menu does not delete the program from your computer.

CHAPTER 7

Have Fun with Windows

Windows 98 offers many fun features. In this chapter you will learn how to play games, videos and music CDs, as well as how to assign sounds to program events in Windows.

PLAY GAMES

Windows includes several games you can play on your computer. Games are a fun way to improve your mouse skills and hand-eye coordination.

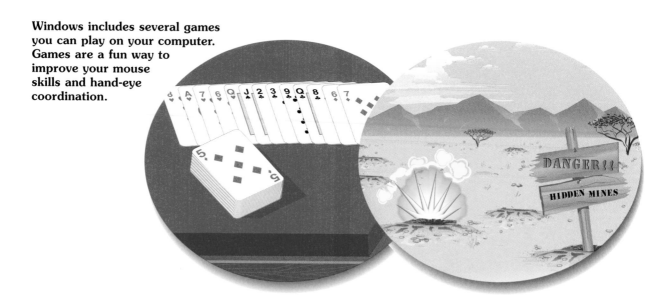

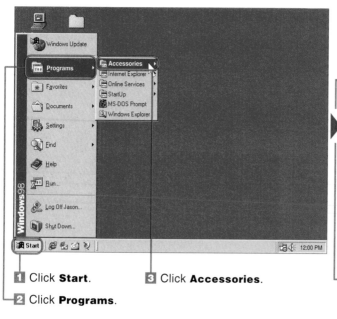

1 Click **Start**.

2 Click **Programs**.

3 Click **Accessories**.

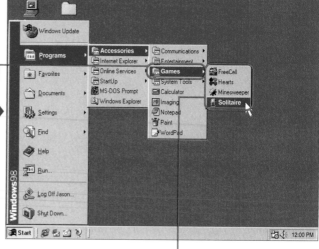

4 Click **Games**.

Note: If **Games** is not available, you must add the Games component to your computer. The Games component is found in the Accessories category. To add a Windows component, see page 178.

5 Click the game you want to play.

Does Windows include any other games?

Windows includes two other card games.

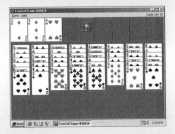

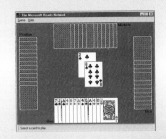

FreeCell

FreeCell is a single-player card game.

Hearts

Hearts is a card game that you can play by yourself or against other people on a network.

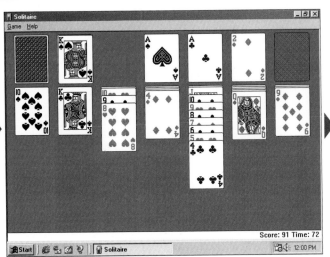

SOLITAIRE

Solitaire is a classic card game that you play on your own. You try to put all the cards in order from ace to king in four stacks, one stack for each suit.

MINESWEEPER

In Minesweeper, you try to locate all of the mines without actually uncovering them.

PLAY A MUSIC CD

You can use your computer to play music CDs while you work.

You need a CD-ROM drive, a sound card and speakers to play music CDs.

■ PLAY A MUSIC CD ■

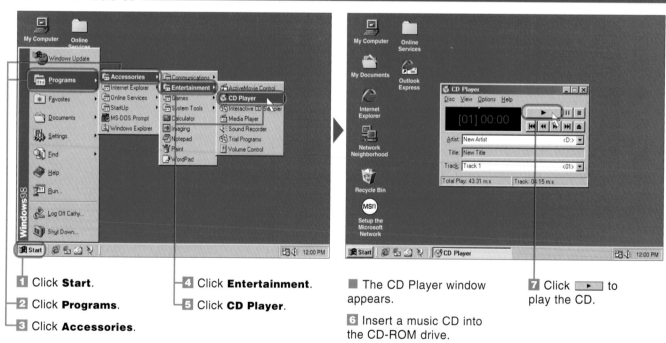

1 Click **Start**.

2 Click **Programs**.

3 Click **Accessories**.

4 Click **Entertainment**.

5 Click **CD Player**.

■ The CD Player window appears.

6 Insert a music CD into the CD-ROM drive.

7 Click ▶ to play the CD.

Can I listen to music privately?

You can listen to music privately by plugging a headset into your CD-ROM drive.

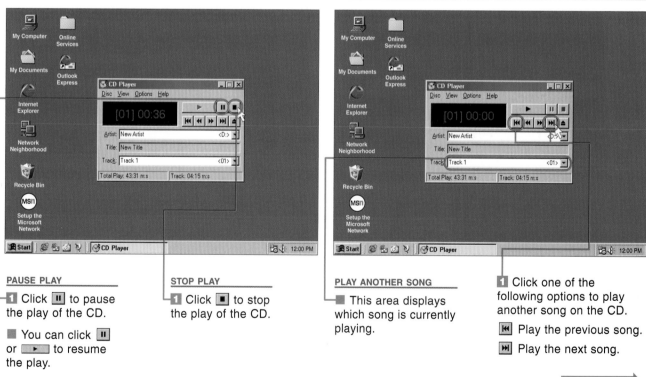

PAUSE PLAY

■1 Click ⏸ to pause the play of the CD.

■ You can click ⏸ or ▶ to resume the play.

STOP PLAY

■1 Click ⏹ to stop the play of the CD.

PLAY ANOTHER SONG

■ This area displays which song is currently playing.

■1 Click one of the following options to play another song on the CD.

⏮ Play the previous song.

⏭ Play the next song.

CONTINUED ▶

PLAY A MUSIC CD

You can have Windows
play the songs on a CD
in random order.

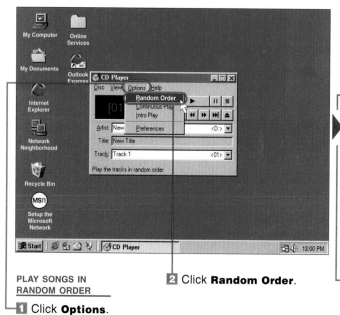

**PLAY SONGS IN
RANDOM ORDER**

1 Click **Options**.

2 Click **Random Order**.

3 Click ▶ to begin
playing the songs in
random order.

*Note: To once again play
the songs in order, repeat
steps 1 and 2.*

CLOSE CD PLAYER

1 When you finish listening
to a CD, click ✕ to close
the CD Player window.

You can easily adjust
the volume of sound
coming from your
speakers.

ADJUST THE VOLUME

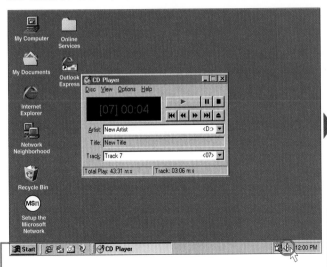

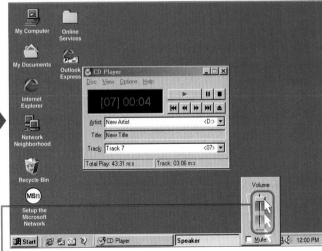

1 Click ◀€ to display
the Volume control.

2 Drag the slider (▭)
up or down to increase
or decrease the volume.

■ To hide the Volume
control, click outside
the box.

ASSIGN SOUNDS TO PROGRAM EVENTS

You can have Windows play sound effects when you perform certain tasks on your computer.

For example, you can hear a tambourine when you empty the Recycle Bin or thunder when you exit Windows.

ASSIGN A SOUND SCHEME

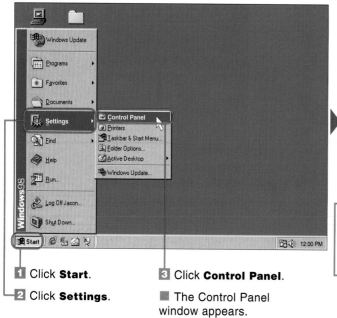

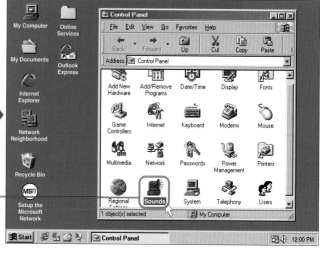

1 Click **Start**.

2 Click **Settings**.

3 Click **Control Panel**.

■ The Control Panel window appears.

4 Double-click **Sounds**.

■ The Sounds Properties dialog box appears.

How can I get more sound schemes?

Windows includes other sound schemes you can install by adding the Multimedia Sound Schemes component, found in the Multimedia category. To add a Windows component, see page 178.

Windows includes these sound schemes:

Jungle   **Musica**   **Robotz**   **Utopia**

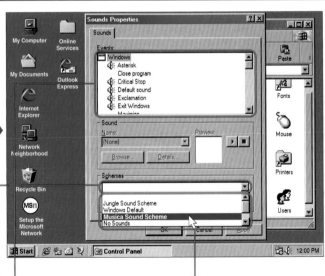

■ This area displays the events to which you can assign sounds.

5 Click this area to display a list of the available sound schemes. Each scheme will change the sounds for many events at once.

6 Click the scheme you want to use.

*Note: A dialog box may appear, asking if you want to save the previous scheme. Click **No** to continue without saving.*

■ A speaker icon 🔊 appears beside each event that will play a sound.

7 To hear the sound an event will play, click the event.

8 Click ▶ to hear the sound.

Note: To adjust the volume of the sound, see page 145.

9 Click **OK** to confirm your selection.

CONTINUED

ASSIGN SOUNDS TO PROGRAM EVENTS

You can assign a sound to an event performed on your computer.

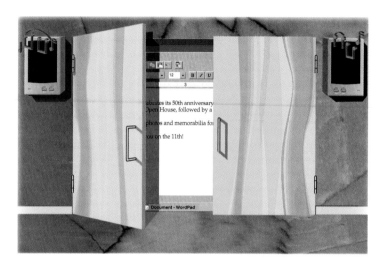

You may want to hear your favorite cartoon character each time you close a program or a sigh of relief when you restore a window. You need a sound card and speakers to hear sounds on your computer.

ASSIGN A SOUND TO ONE EVENT

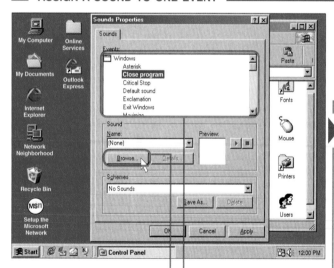

1 Display the Sounds Properties dialog box.

Note: To display the Sounds Properties dialog box, perform steps 1 to 4 on page 146.

2 Click the event to which you want to assign a sound.

3 Click **Browse** to find the sound you want to use on your computer.

■ The Browse dialog box appears.

■ This area shows the location of the displayed sound files. You can click this area to change the location.

4 Click the sound you want to hear every time the event occurs.

Where can I get sounds?

You can purchase sounds
at computer stores or get
sounds on the Internet.
Make sure you use sounds
with the .wav extension,
such as wolfhowl.wav.

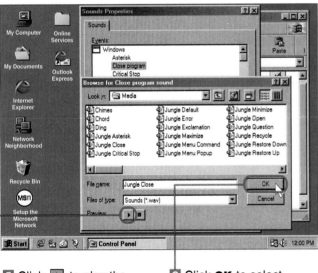

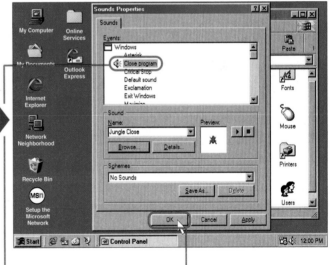

■5 Click ▶ to play the
sound you selected.

■6 Click **OK** to select
the sound.

■ A speaker icon (◀€)
appears beside the
event.

■7 To assign sounds
to other events, repeat
steps **2** to **6** for each
event.

■8 Click **OK** to confirm
your changes.

PLAY VIDEOS

You can play videos
on your computer.

PLAY VIDEOS

1 Double-click the video
you want to play.

■ A window appears and
the video starts to play.

■ This area displays the
total length of the video
and the current position
in the video.

2 Click one of these
options to pause (■)
or stop (■) the play
of the video.

150

?

Where can I get videos?

The Windows 98 CD-ROM disc includes several videos you can play. You can also get videos on the Internet or purchase videos at computer stores. Windows can play different types of videos, including videos with the .avi and .mpg extensions (example: film.mpg).

3 Click ▶ to once again play the video.

4 To move through the video, position the mouse ⏳ over the slider (▯) and then drag the slider to a new location.

5 When you finish playing the video, click ☒ to close the window.

CHAPTER 8

Optimize Your Computer

There are many improvements you can make to optimize your computer. In this chapter you will learn how to complete important tasks, such as repairing disk errors and deleting unnecessary files.

FORMAT A FLOPPY DISK

You must format a floppy disk before you can use the disk to store information.

Floppy disks you buy at computer stores are usually formatted. You may want to later format a disk to erase the information it contains and prepare the disk for storing new information.

FORMAT A FLOPPY DISK

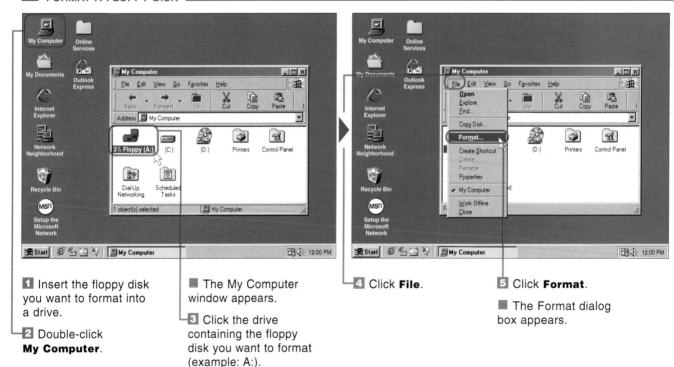

1 Insert the floppy disk you want to format into a drive.

2 Double-click **My Computer**.

■ The My Computer window appears.

3 Click the drive containing the floppy disk you want to format (example: A:).

4 Click **File**.

5 Click **Format**.

■ The Format dialog box appears.

How can I tell how much information a floppy disk can store?

Double-Density 720 KB

A 3.5-inch floppy disk that has one hole can store 720 KB of information.

High-Density 1.44 MB

A 3.5-inch floppy disk that has two holes and displays the HD symbol can store 1.44 MB of information.

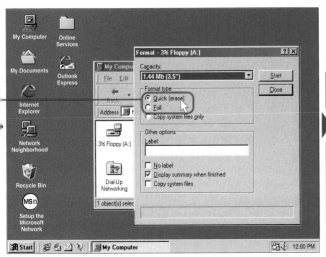

6 Click the type of format you want to perform (○ changes to ⊙).

Note: If the floppy disk has never been formatted, select the Full option.

Quick (erase)
Removes all files but does not scan the disk for damaged areas.

Full
Removes all files and scans the disk for damaged areas.

7 Click this area to specify how much information the floppy disk can store.

8 Click the storage capacity of the floppy disk.

CONTINUED

FORMAT A FLOPPY DISK

Before formatting a floppy disk, make sure the disk does not contain information you may need. Formatting a floppy disk will permanently remove all the information on the disk.

FORMAT A FLOPPY DISK (CONTINUED)

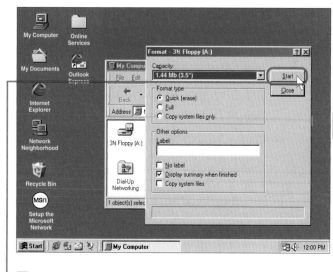

9 Click **Start** to start formatting the floppy disk.

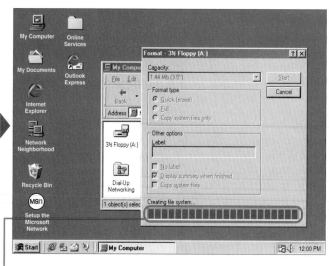

■ This area displays the progress of the format.

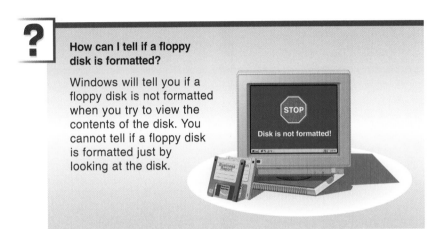

How can I tell if a floppy disk is formatted?

Windows will tell you if a floppy disk is not formatted when you try to view the contents of the disk. You cannot tell if a floppy disk is formatted just by looking at the disk.

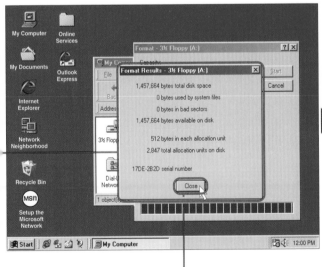

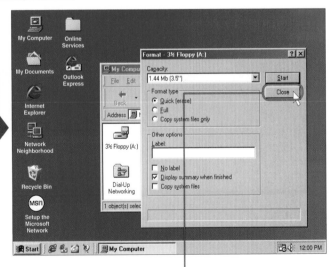

■ The Format Results dialog box appears when the format is complete. The dialog box displays information about the formatted disk.

10 When you finish viewing the information, click **Close** to close the dialog box.

■ To format another floppy disk, insert the disk and then repeat steps 6 to 10 starting on page 155.

11 Click **Close** to close the Format dialog box.

VIEW AMOUNT OF DISK SPACE

You can view the
amount of used and
free space on a disk.

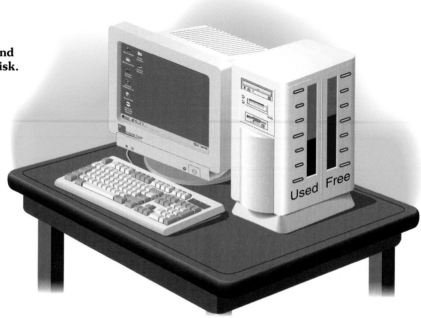

VIEW AMOUNT OF DISK SPACE

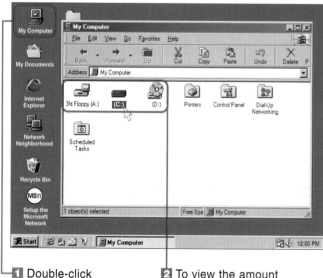

1 Double-click
My Computer.

■ The My Computer
window appears.

2 To view the amount
of space on a disk, click
the disk of interest
(example: C:).

*Note: To view the amount of space
on a floppy disk, you need to first
insert the disk into the drive.*

3 Click **File**.

4 Click **Properties**.

■ The Properties dialog
box appears.

How can I increase the amount of free space on my hard disk?

Delete files you no longer need. See page 88 to delete files.

Use Disk Cleanup to remove unnecessary files from your computer. See page 168 to use Disk Cleanup.

Copy files you rarely use to a floppy disk and then delete the files from your computer. See page 86 to copy files to a floppy disk.

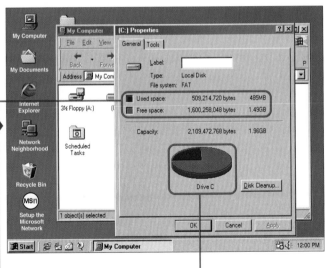

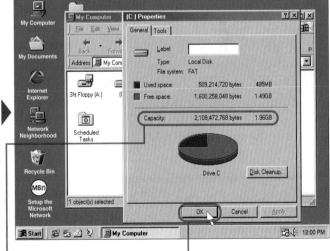

■ This area displays the amount of used and free space on the disk in bytes, megabytes (MB) and gigabytes (GB).

■ A pie chart visually indicates the amount of used and free space on the disk.

■ This area displays the total disk storage space, in both bytes and gigabytes (GB).

5 When you finish viewing the information, click **OK** to close the Properties dialog box.

DETECT AND REPAIR DISK ERRORS

You can improve the performance of your computer by using ScanDisk to detect and repair hard disk errors.

The hard disk is the primary device a computer uses to store information.

DETECT AND REPAIR DISK ERRORS

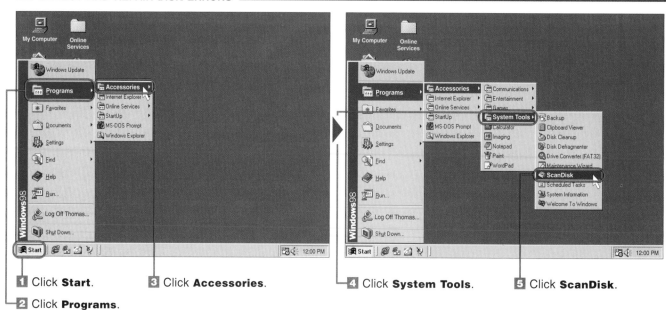

1 Click **Start**.

2 Click **Programs**.

3 Click **Accessories**.

4 Click **System Tools**.

5 Click **ScanDisk**.

?

How often should I check my hard disk for errors?

You should check your hard disk for errors at least once a month. You can set up Windows to check for hard disk errors and perform other tasks on a regular basis. See page 174.

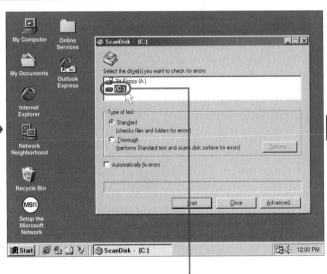

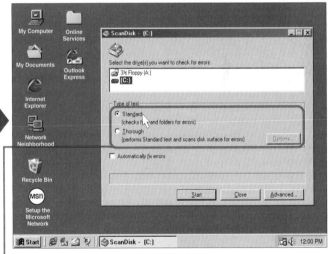

■ The ScanDisk window appears.

6 Click the disk you want to check for errors (example: C:).

7 Click the type of test you want to perform (○ changes to ⦿).

Standard
Checks files and folders for errors.

Thorough
Checks files, folders and the disk surface for errors.

CONTINUED ▶

DETECT AND REPAIR DISK ERRORS

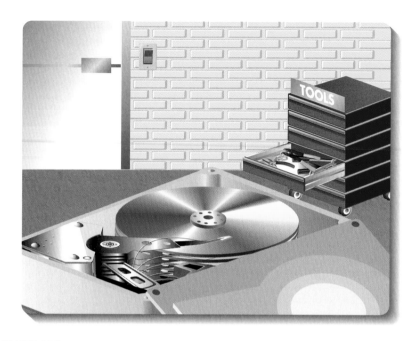

You can have Windows
automatically repair any
disk errors it finds.

DETECT AND REPAIR DISK ERRORS (CONTINUED)

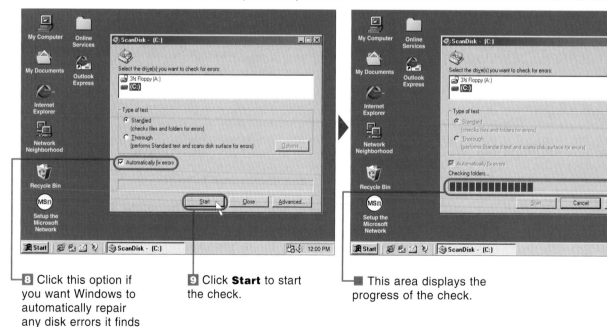

8 Click this option if
you want Windows to
automatically repair
any disk errors it finds
(☐ changes to ☑).

9 Click **Start** to start
the check.

■ This area displays the
progress of the check.

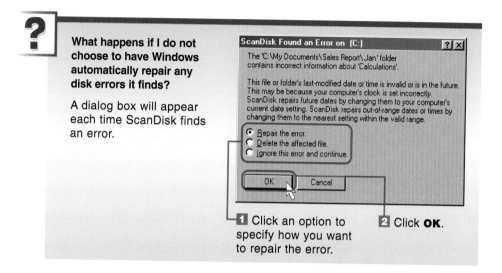

What happens if I do not choose to have Windows automatically repair any disk errors it finds?

A dialog box will appear each time ScanDisk finds an error.

■1 Click an option to specify how you want to repair the error.

■2 Click **OK**.

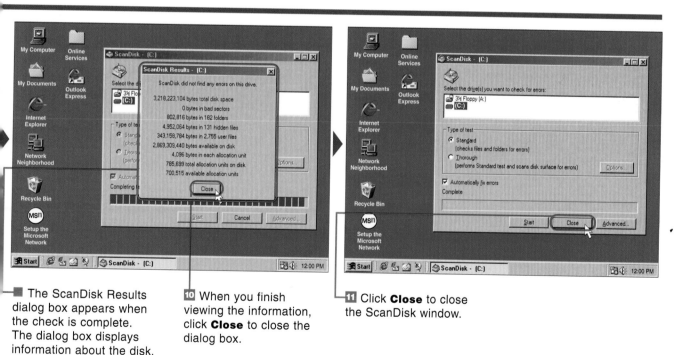

■ The ScanDisk Results dialog box appears when the check is complete. The dialog box displays information about the disk.

■10 When you finish viewing the information, click **Close** to close the dialog box.

■11 Click **Close** to close the ScanDisk window.

DEFRAGMENT YOUR HARD DISK

You can improve
the performance of
your computer by
defragmenting your
hard disk.

A fragmented hard disk
stores parts of a file in
many different locations.
Your computer must
search many areas on
the disk to retrieve a file.

DEFRAGMENT YOUR HARD DISK

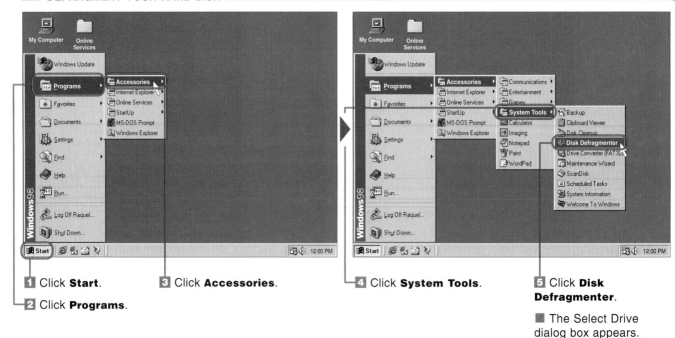

1 Click **Start**.

2 Click **Programs**.

3 Click **Accessories**.

4 Click **System Tools**.

5 Click **Disk Defragmenter**.

■ The Select Drive
dialog box appears.

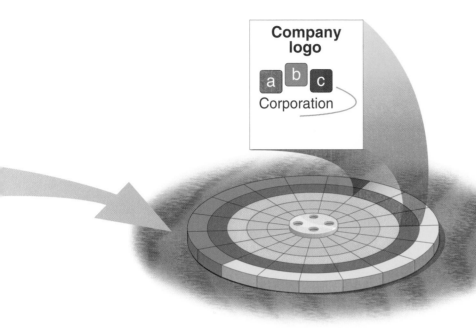

You can use Disk Defragmenter to place all the parts of a file in one location. This reduces the time your computer will spend locating the file.

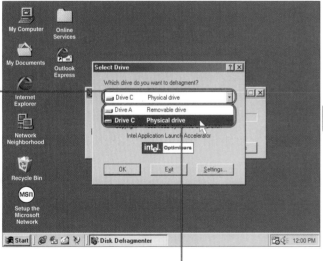

6 Click this area to display a list of the drives you can defragment.

7 Click the drive you want to defragment.

8 Click **OK** to start the defragmentation.

CONTINUED

DEFRAGMENT YOUR HARD DISK

You can perform other tasks on your computer while Windows defragments your hard disk, but your computer will operate slower and the defragmentation will take longer.

The defragmentation process must restart each time a program stores information on your hard disk. You may want to close all other programs to speed up the defragmentation.

■ DEFRAGMENT YOUR HARD DISK (CONTINUED) ■

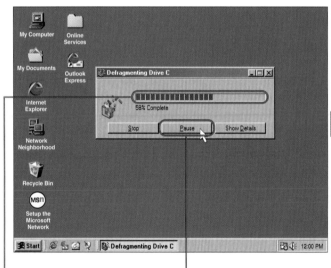

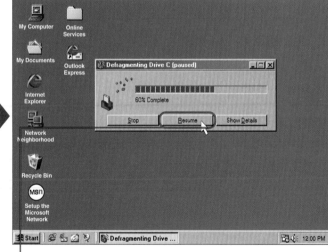

■ The Defragmenting Drive window appears.

■ This area displays the progress of the defragmentation.

9 To temporarily stop the defragmentation so you can perform other tasks at full speed, click **Pause**.

10 To resume the defragmentation, click **Resume**.

How often should I defragment my hard disk?

You should defragment your hard disk at least once a month. You can set up Windows to defragment your hard disk and perform other computer maintenance tasks on a regular basis. See page 174.

■ A dialog box appears when the defragmentation is complete.

11 Click **Yes** to close Disk Defragmenter.

■ You can now use your computer as usual.

USING DISK CLEANUP

Disk Cleanup will remove unnecessary files from your computer to free up disk space.

USING DISK CLEANUP

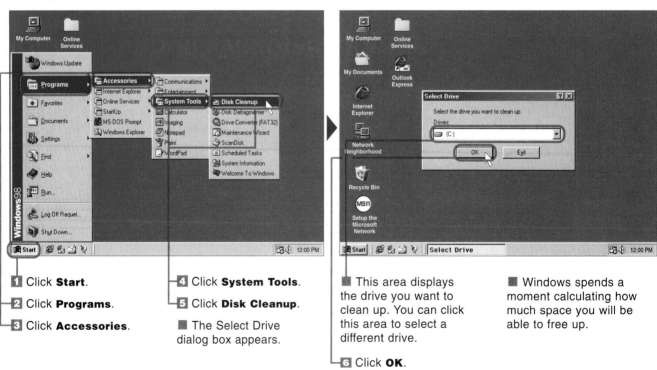

1 Click **Start**.

2 Click **Programs**.

3 Click **Accessories**.

4 Click **System Tools**.

5 Click **Disk Cleanup**.

■ The Select Drive dialog box appears.

■ This area displays the drive you want to clean up. You can click this area to select a different drive.

6 Click **OK**.

■ Windows spends a moment calculating how much space you will be able to free up.

?

What types of files can Disk Cleanup remove?

Temporary Internet Files
Web pages stored on your computer for quick viewing.

Downloaded Program Files
Information transferred from the Internet when you view certain Web pages.

Recycle Bin
Files you have deleted.

Temporary Files
Files created by programs for storing temporary information.

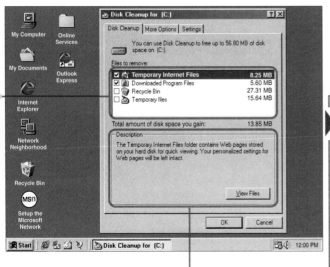

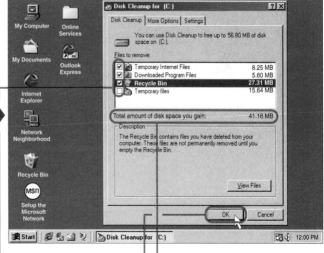

■ The Disk Cleanup dialog box appears.

◢ This area displays the types of files you can remove and the amount of disk space taken up by each file type.

■ This area displays a description of the highlighted file type.

7 Windows will remove the files for each file type that displays a check mark (☑). You can click the box (☐) beside a file type to add or remove the check mark.

■ This area displays the total space Windows will free up from the file types you selected.

8 Click **OK** to remove the files.

■ A confirmation dialog box appears. Click **Yes** to permanently delete the files.

SCHEDULE TASKS

You can use Task Scheduler to have Windows automatically perform tasks on a regular basis. This is useful for running computer maintenance programs such as Disk Defragmenter or ScanDisk.

SCHEDULE TASKS

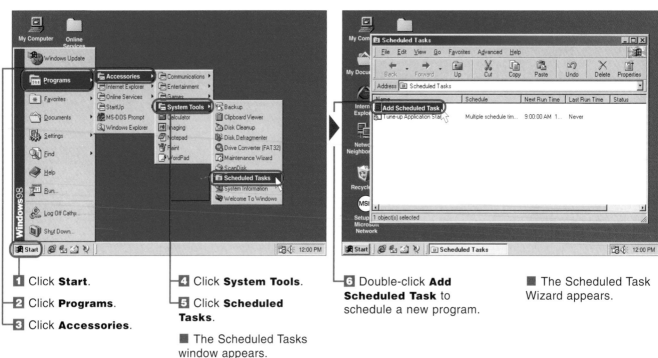

1 Click **Start**.

2 Click **Programs**.

3 Click **Accessories**.

4 Click **System Tools**.

5 Click **Scheduled Tasks**.

■ The Scheduled Tasks window appears.

6 Double-click **Add Scheduled Task** to schedule a new program.

■ The Scheduled Task Wizard appears.

How does Task Scheduler know when to start a program?

Task Scheduler uses the date and time set in your computer to determine when to start a scheduled task. Before you schedule a task, make sure this information is correct. See page 110 to change the date and time set in your computer.

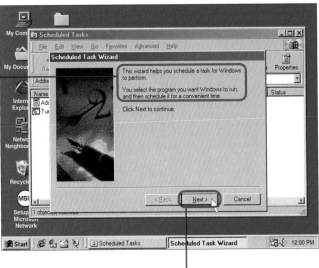

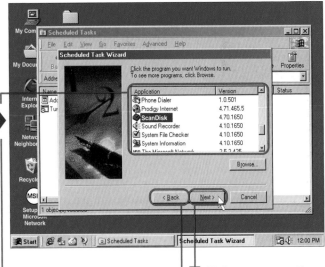

■ This area provides information about the wizard.

7 Click **Next** to continue.

■ This area lists the programs installed on your computer.

8 Click the program you want to schedule.

9 Click **Next** to continue.

■ You can click **Back** at any time to return to a previous step and change your answers.

CONTINUED

SCHEDULE TASKS

You can specify the date
and time you want Task
Scheduler to start a
program. Schedule a
program during a time
when your computer
will be turned on.

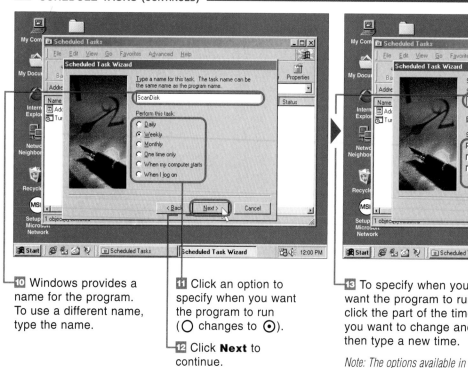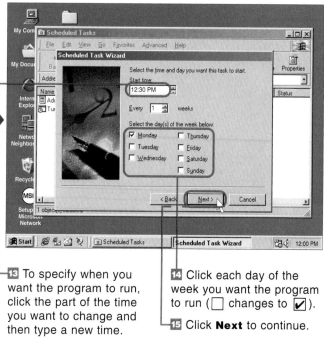

10 Windows provides a
name for the program.
To use a different name,
type the name.

11 Click an option to
specify when you want
the program to run
(○ changes to ⦿).

12 Click **Next** to
continue.

13 To specify when you
want the program to run,
click the part of the time
you want to change and
then type a new time.

*Note: The options available in
this screen depend on the option
you selected in step 11.*

14 Click each day of the
week you want the program
to run (☐ changes to ☑).

15 Click **Next** to continue.

Can I remove a task so it will no longer run automatically?

To remove a task so Windows will no longer run the task automatically, click the program in the Scheduled Tasks window and then press the `Delete` key. Then click **Yes** to confirm the deletion. Deleting a program from Task Scheduler does not remove the program from your computer.

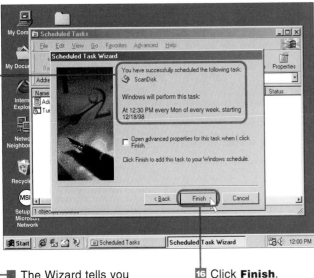

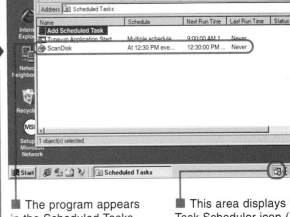

■ The Wizard tells you that you have successfully added the program to Task Scheduler and provides information about when the program will run.

16 Click **Finish**.

■ The program appears in the Scheduled Tasks window.

17 You can click ✕ to close the window.

■ This area displays the Task Scheduler icon (🖳). You can double-click this icon to redisplay the Scheduled Tasks window at any time.

USING THE MAINTENANCE WIZARD

You can schedule regular maintenance tasks to optimize the performance of your computer.

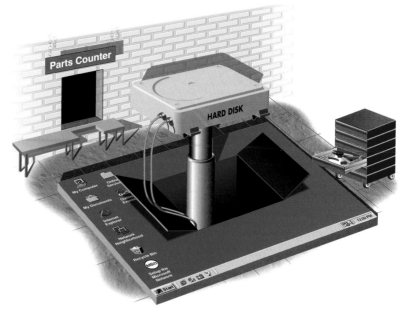

USING THE MAINTENANCE WIZARD

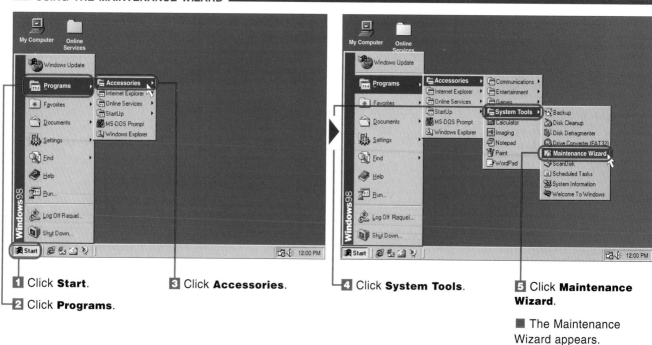

1 Click **Start**.

2 Click **Programs**.

3 Click **Accessories**.

4 Click **System Tools**.

5 Click **Maintenance Wizard**.

■ The Maintenance Wizard appears.

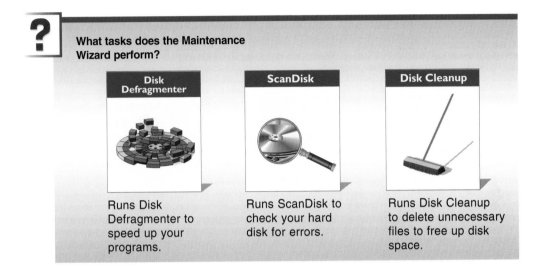

What tasks does the Maintenance Wizard perform?

Disk Defragmenter

Runs Disk Defragmenter to speed up your programs.

ScanDisk

Runs ScanDisk to check your hard disk for errors.

Disk Cleanup

Runs Disk Cleanup to delete unnecessary files to free up disk space.

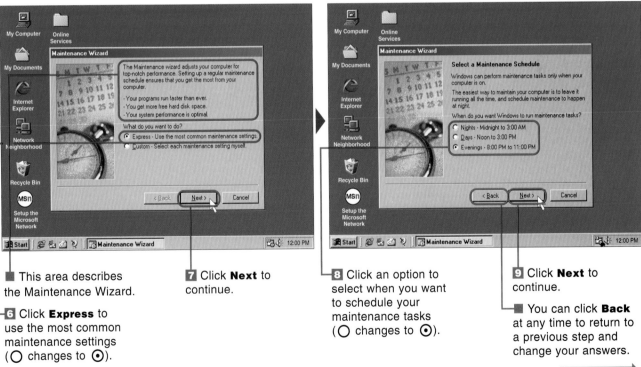

■ This area describes the Maintenance Wizard.

6 Click **Express** to use the most common maintenance settings (○ changes to ⊙).

7 Click **Next** to continue.

8 Click an option to select when you want to schedule your maintenance tasks (○ changes to ⊙).

9 Click **Next** to continue.

■ You can click **Back** at any time to return to a previous step and change your answers.

CONTINUED

USING THE MAINTENANCE WIZARD

Your computer must be on when the scheduled maintenance tasks will run.

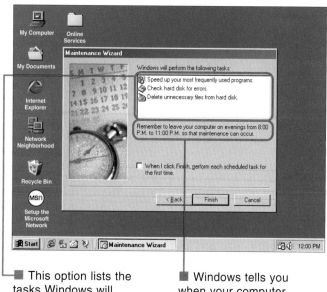

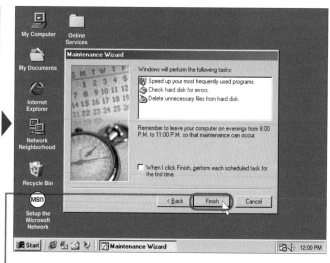

■ This option lists the tasks Windows will perform.

■ Windows tells you when your computer must be on for the maintenance to occur.

■**10** Click **Finish** to finish scheduling the maintenance tasks.

■ Windows will now run the tasks at the scheduled time.

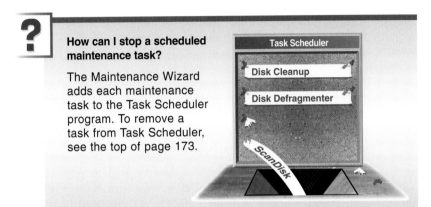

How can I stop a scheduled maintenance task?

The Maintenance Wizard adds each maintenance task to the Task Scheduler program. To remove a task from Task Scheduler, see the top of page 173.

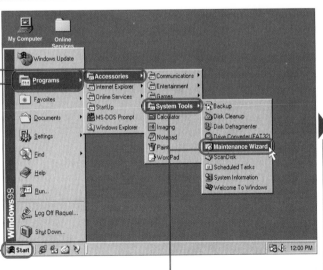

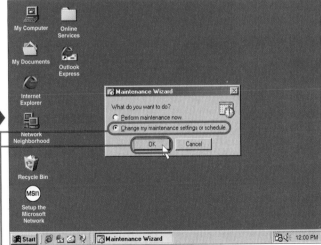

CHANGE MAINTENANCE SETTINGS

■1 Click **Start**.

■2 Click **Programs**.

■3 Click **Accessories**.

■4 Click **System Tools**.

■5 Click **Maintenance Wizard**.

■ The Maintenance Wizard dialog box appears.

■6 Click this option to change your maintenance settings (○ changes to ⊙).

■7 Click **OK**.

■ The Maintenance Wizard appears.

■8 Perform steps 6 to 10 starting on page 175 to change your maintenance settings.

ADD WINDOWS COMPONENTS

You can add components
to your computer that were
not added when you first
set up Windows.

EXTRA Windows Components

When setting up Windows,
most people do not install
all the components that
come with the program.
This prevents unneeded
components from taking
up storage space on the
computer.

■■ ADD WINDOWS COMPONENTS ■■

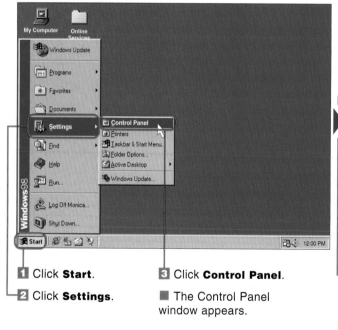

1 Click **Start**.

2 Click **Settings**.

3 Click **Control Panel**.

■ The Control Panel
window appears.

4 Double-click
Add/Remove Programs.

■ The Add/Remove
Programs Properties
dialog box appears.

**Which Windows components
can I add to my computer?**

Some Windows
components you
can add to your
computer include:

Games
Provides entertaining
games such as
Minesweeper and
Solitaire.

Desktop Themes
Allows you to
customize your
desktop with a
particular theme,
such as a baseball
or jungle theme.

**Multimedia Sound
Schemes**
Provides sound effects
Windows can play
when you perform
certain tasks on your
computer.

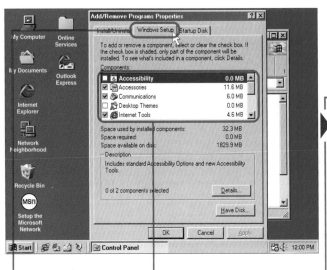

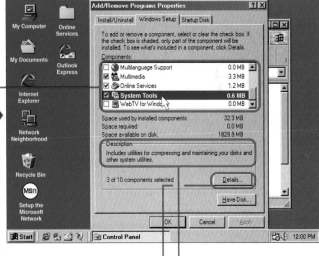

■5 Click the **Windows
Setup** tab.

*Note: Windows may take
a moment to display the
information.*

■ This area displays the
categories of components
you can add to your
computer.

■ The box beside each
category indicates if all (✔),
some (✔) or none (☐)
of the components in the
category exist on your
computer.

■6 Click a category to
display a description of
the components in the
category.

■ This area displays
a description of the
components in the
category.

■7 Click **Details** to
display the components
in the category.

CONTINUED

ADD WINDOWS COMPONENTS

When adding Windows components, you will be asked to insert the CD-ROM disc you used to install Windows.

ADD WINDOWS COMPONENTS (CONTINUED)

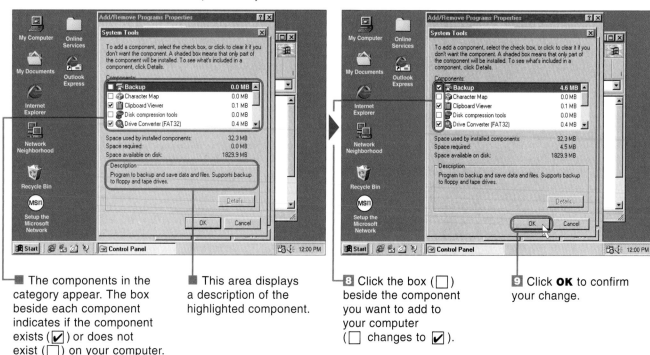

■ The components in the category appear. The box beside each component indicates if the component exists (☑) or does not exist (☐) on your computer.

■ This area displays a description of the highlighted component.

8 Click the box (☐) beside the component you want to add to your computer (☐ changes to ☑).

9 Click **OK** to confirm your change.

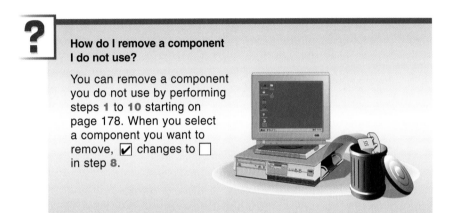

How do I remove a component I do not use?

You can remove a component you do not use by performing steps **1** to **10** starting on page 178. When you select a component you want to remove, ☑ changes to ☐ in step **8**.

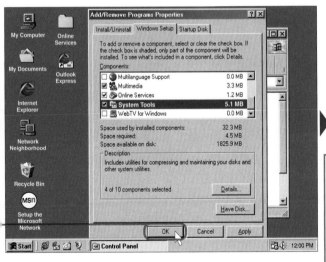

-**10** Click **OK** to close the Add/Remove Programs Properties dialog box.

■ The Insert Disk dialog box appears, asking you to insert the Windows 98 CD-ROM disc.

11 Insert the CD-ROM disc into the drive.

12 Click **OK** to continue.

■ Windows copies the necessary files to your computer.

Note: Windows may ask you to restart your computer.

INSTALL A PRINTER

Before you can use a new printer, you need to install the printer on your computer. Windows includes a wizard that guides you step-by-step through the process of installing a new printer.

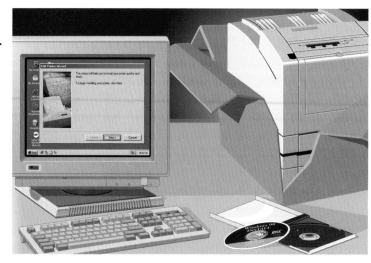

You will need the Windows 98 CD-ROM disc to install a new printer.

■ INSTALL A PRINTER ■

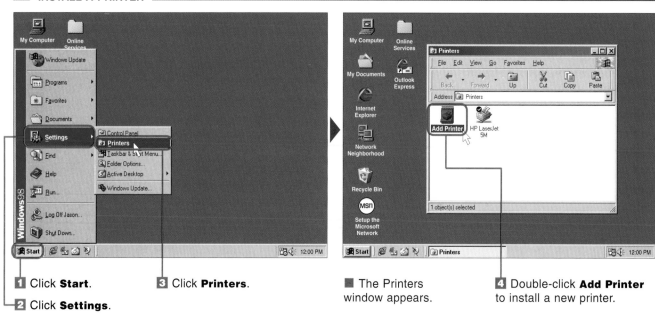

1 Click **Start**.

2 Click **Settings**.

3 Click **Printers**.

■ The Printers window appears.

4 Double-click **Add Printer** to install a new printer.

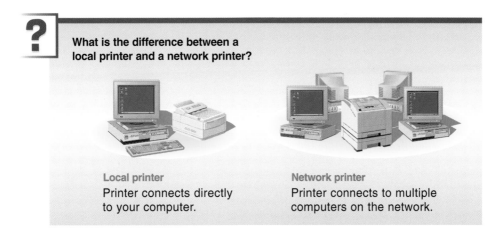

What is the difference between a local printer and a network printer?

Local printer
Printer connects directly to your computer.

Network printer
Printer connects to multiple computers on the network.

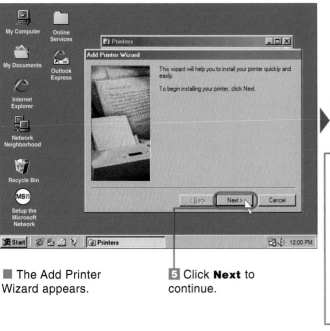

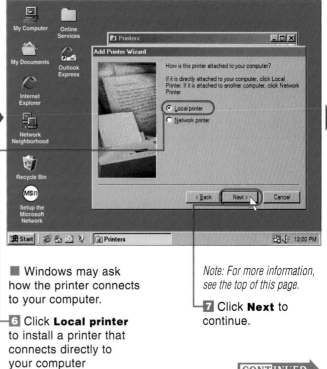

■ The Add Printer Wizard appears.

5 Click **Next** to continue.

■ Windows may ask how the printer connects to your computer.

6 Click **Local printer** to install a printer that connects directly to your computer (○ changes to ⊙).

Note: For more information, see the top of this page.

7 Click **Next** to continue.

CONTINUED

INSTALL A PRINTER

When installing a printer, you must specify the manufacturer and model of the printer.

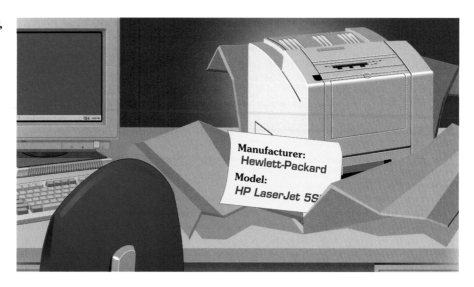

INSTALL A PRINTER (CONTINUED)

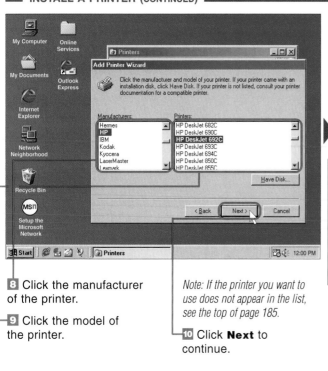

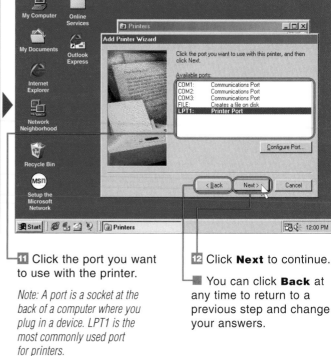

8 Click the manufacturer of the printer.

9 Click the model of the printer.

Note: If the printer you want to use does not appear in the list, see the top of page 185.

10 Click **Next** to continue.

11 Click the port you want to use with the printer.

Note: A port is a socket at the back of a computer where you plug in a device. LPT1 is the most commonly used port for printers.

12 Click **Next** to continue.

■ You can click **Back** at any time to return to a previous step and change your answers.

What if the printer I want to install does not appear in the list?

If the printer you want to install does not appear in the list, you can use the installation disk(s) that came with the printer.

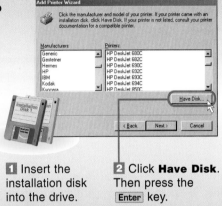

1 Insert the installation disk into the drive.

2 Click **Have Disk**. Then press the Enter key.

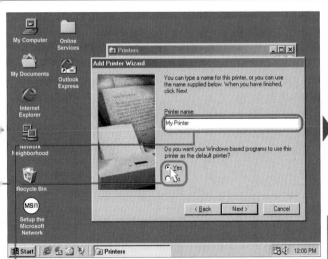

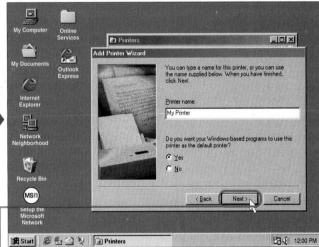

13 Windows provides a name for the printer. To use a different name, type the name.

14 Click one of these options to specify if you want to use the printer as the default printer (○ changes to ⊙).

Yes
Files will always print to this printer.

No
Files will print to this printer only when you select the printer.

15 Click **Next** to continue.

CONTINUED

INSTALL A PRINTER

Windows will ask if you want to print a test page to confirm that your printer is installed properly.

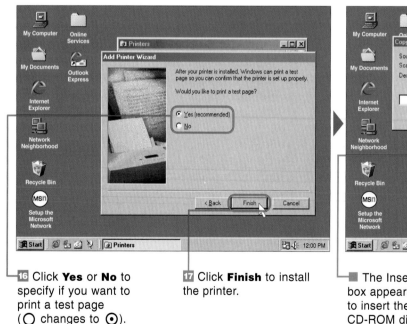

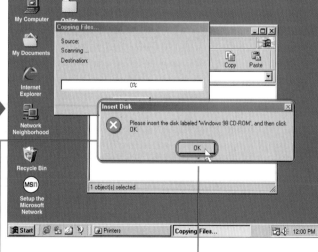

16 Click **Yes** or **No** to specify if you want to print a test page (◯ changes to ◉).

17 Click **Finish** to install the printer.

■ The Insert Disk dialog box appears, asking you to insert the Windows 98 CD-ROM disc.

18 Insert the CD-ROM disc into the drive.

19 Click **OK** to continue.

■ Windows copies the necessary files to your computer.

?

Why do I need the Windows CD-ROM disc to install a printer?

Your computer needs special software, called a driver, to be able to use a new printer. A driver is a program that allows your computer to communicate with the printer. The Windows 98 CD-ROM disc includes the most popular drivers.

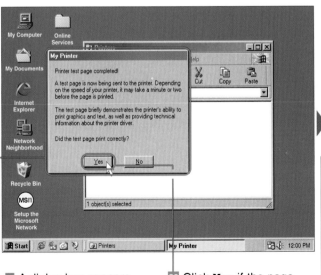

■ A dialog box appears, asking if the test page printed correctly.

*Note: This dialog box does not appear if you selected **No** in step **16**.*

20 Click **Yes** if the page printed correctly.

■ An icon for the printer appears in the Printers window.

21 Click **X** to close the Printers window.

INSTALL NEW HARDWARE

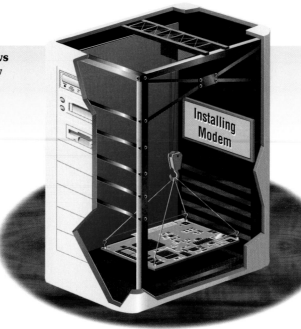

You can have Windows
detect and install new
hardware for you.

Installing
Modem

You can add hardware such
as a mouse, keyboard or
modem. To install a printer,
see page 182.

■ INSTALL NEW HARDWARE ■

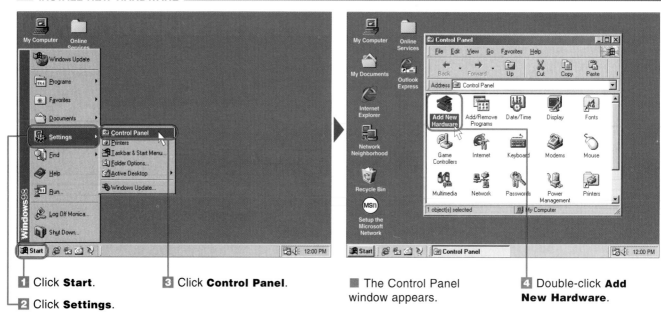

1 Click **Start**.

2 Click **Settings**.

3 Click **Control Panel**.

■ The Control Panel
window appears.

4 Double-click **Add
New Hardware**.

What are Plug and Play devices?

Plug and Play devices are devices that Windows can automatically set up to work properly with your computer, which makes them easy to install. When purchasing a new device for your computer, you should try to purchase a Plug and Play device.

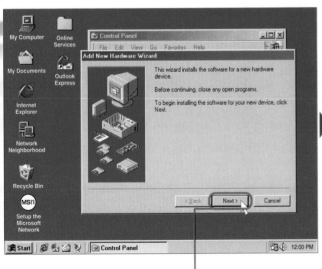

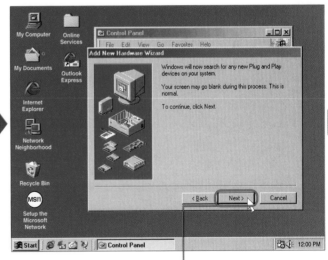

■ The Add New Hardware Wizard appears.

■ Windows tells you to close any open programs before continuing.

5 Click **Next** to begin installing the new hardware.

■ The wizard informs you that Windows will search for any new Plug and Play devices on your computer.

6 Click **Next** to have Windows search for any new Plug and Play devices.

CONTINUED

INSTALL NEW HARDWARE

The wizard guides you step-by-step through the installation, first detecting the hardware and then installing the software needed by the hardware.

Hardware Detected

INSTALL NEW HARDWARE (CONTINUED)

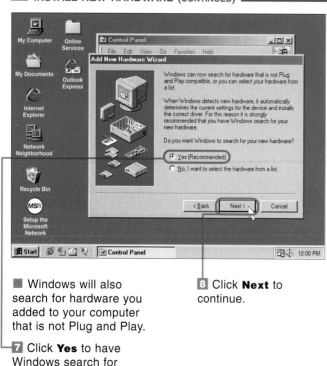

■ Windows will also search for hardware you added to your computer that is not Plug and Play.

7 Click **Yes** to have Windows search for hardware that is not Plug and Play (○ changes to ⊙).

8 Click **Next** to continue.

■ Windows is ready to search for new hardware that is not Plug and Play.

9 Click **Next** to start searching for the new hardware.

■ This area displays the progress of the search. The search may take several minutes.

*Note: You can click **Cancel** to stop the search at any time.*

190

? **Is there hardware I can install that will make typing more comfortable?**

You may want to purchase and install an ergonomic keyboard. Ergonomic keyboards position your hands naturally and support your wrists so you can work more comfortably at your computer.

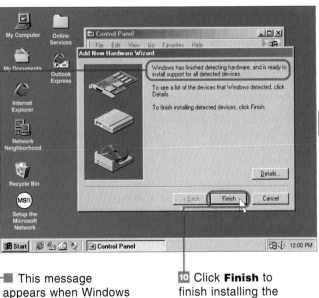

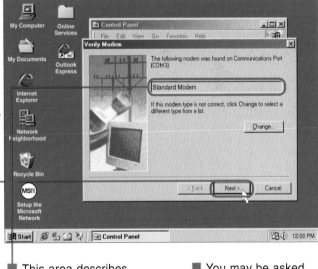

◀ This message appears when Windows has finished searching for the new hardware.

10 Click **Finish** to finish installing the new hardware.

■ This area describes the hardware Windows found.

11 Click **Next** to continue.

■ You may be asked to insert the Windows CD-ROM disc and restart your computer.

■ You can now use your new hardware.

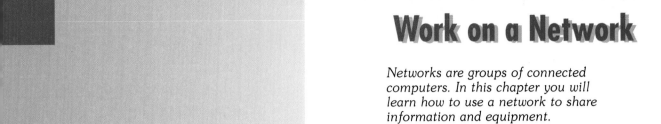

CHAPTER 9

Work on a Network

Networks are groups of connected computers. In this chapter you will learn how to use a network to share information and equipment.

INTRODUCTION TO NETWORKS

A network is a group of connected computers that allow people to share information and equipment.

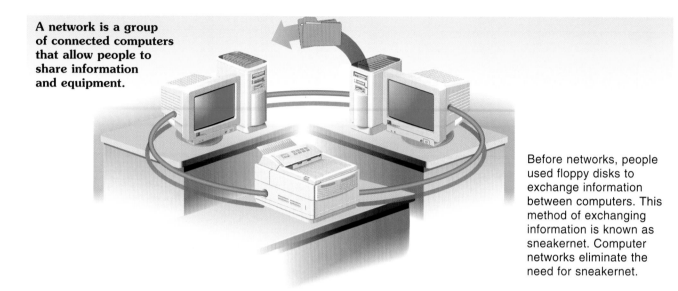

Before networks, people used floppy disks to exchange information between computers. This method of exchanging information is known as sneakernet. Computer networks eliminate the need for sneakernet.

Share Information

Networks let you easily share data and programs. You can exchange documents, spreadsheets, pictures and electronic mail between computers.

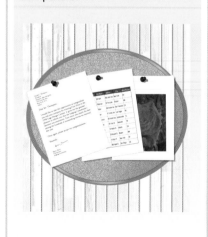

Share Equipment

Computers connected to a network can share equipment, such as a printer, to reduce costs. For example, rather than buying a printer for each person on a network, everyone can share one central printer.

Workgroups

Each computer on a network belongs to a workgroup. Small companies usually have one workgroup. Large companies have many workgroups to better organize information and resources.

TURN ON SHARING

Before you can share information or a printer with individuals on a network, you must set up your computer to share resources.

TURN ON SHARING

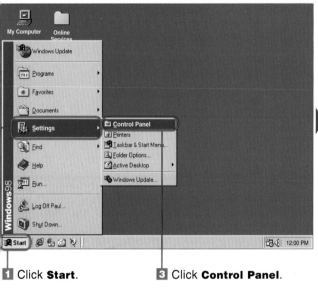

1 Click **Start**.

2 Click **Settings**.

3 Click **Control Panel**.

■ The Control Panel window appears.

4 Double-click **Network**.

■ The Network dialog box appears.

CONTINUED

TURN ON SHARING

Windows requires you to restart your computer before the new sharing settings will take effect.

Make sure you close any open programs before restarting your computer.

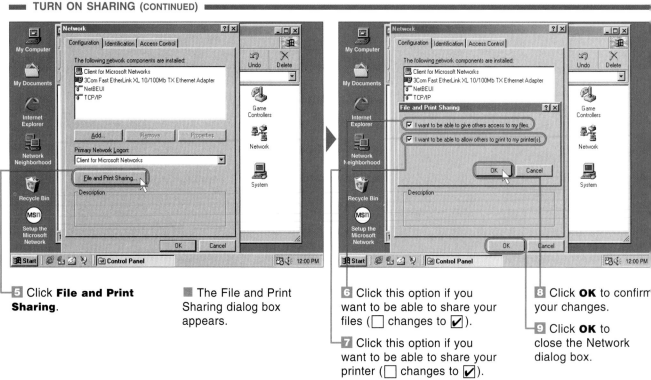

5 Click **File and Print Sharing**.

■ The File and Print Sharing dialog box appears.

6 Click this option if you want to be able to share your files (☐ changes to ☑).

7 Click this option if you want to be able to share your printer (☐ changes to ☑).

8 Click **OK** to confirm your changes.

9 Click **OK** to close the Network dialog box.

? I turned on sharing, but my colleagues still cannot access my files and printer. What is wrong?

Once you set up your computer to share information or a printer, you must specify exactly what you want to share. To specify the information you want to share, see page 198. To specify the printer you want to share, see page 202.

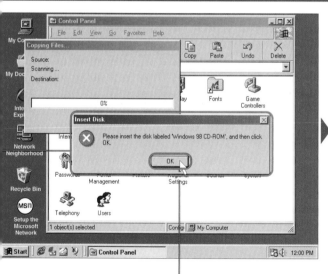

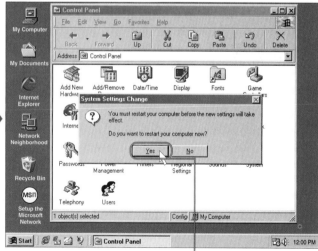

■ The Insert Disk dialog box appears, asking you to insert the Windows CD-ROM disc.

10 Insert the disc into your CD-ROM drive.

11 Click **OK** to continue.

■ Windows copies the necessary files to your computer.

■ The System Settings Change dialog box appears, telling you that Windows needs to restart your computer before the new settings will take effect.

12 Click **Yes** to restart your computer.

■ To turn off file and printer sharing, repeat steps **1** to **12** starting on page 195 (☑ changes to ☐ in steps **6** and **7**).

SHARE INFORMATION

You can specify exactly what information you want to share with individuals on a network.

You must turn on sharing before you can share information. To turn on sharing, see page 195.

■ SHARE INFORMATION ■

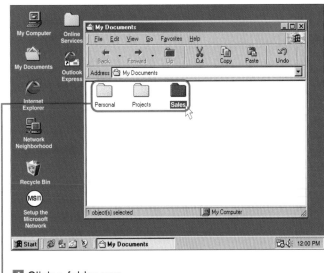

1 Click a folder you want to share.

2 Click **File**.

3 Click **Sharing**.

■ The Properties dialog box appears.

How can I stop sharing a folder?

To stop sharing a folder, repeat steps **1** to **4** starting on page 198, selecting **Not Shared** in step **4**. Then click **OK** in the Properties dialog box to confirm your change.

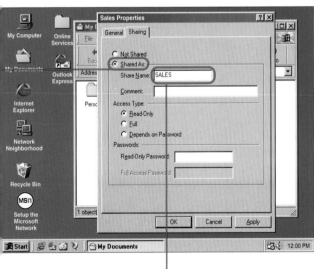

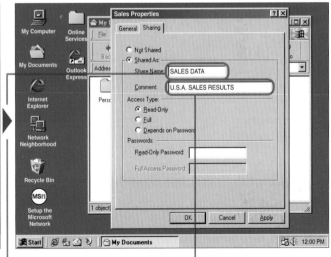

■4 Click **Shared As:** to share the folder with others on a network (○ changes to ⊙).

■ This area displays the name of the folder individuals will see on the network.

■5 If you want to give the folder a different name, drag the mouse I over the text until the text is highlighted. Then type a new name.

■6 Click this area to enter a comment about the folder. Then type the comment.

CONTINUED

SHARE INFORMATION

You can give individuals on a network one of three types of access to your information.

Read-Only
All individuals on the network can read but cannot change or delete information.

SHARE INFORMATION (CONTINUED)

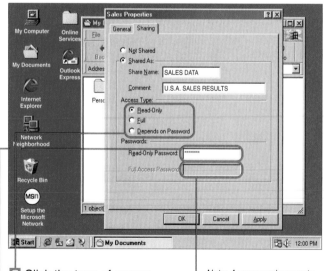

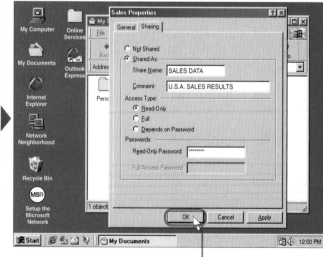

7 Click the type of access you want to assign to the folder (○ changes to ⊙).

8 If you selected Read-Only access and want to assign a password, click this area and type a password.

Note: A password prevents unauthorized people from accessing the folder.

9 If you selected Full access and want to assign a password, click this area and type a password.

■ If you selected Depends on Password access, perform steps **8** and **9** to enter both a Read-Only and a Full Access password.

10 Click **OK** to confirm your selections.

Full

All individuals on the network can read, change and delete information.

Depends on Password

Some individuals on the network have Read-Only access, while others have Full access, depending on which password they enter.

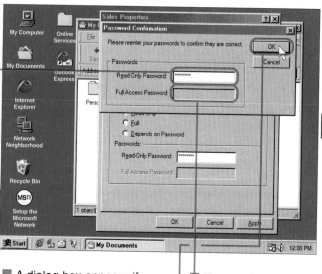

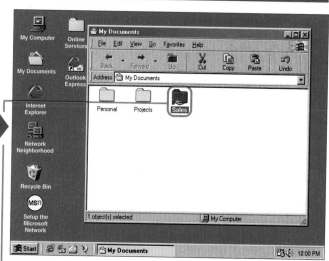

■ A dialog box appears if you entered a password.

11 Retype the password to confirm the password.

■ If you selected Depends on Password access, press the `Tab` key and then retype the Full Access password.

12 Click **OK**.

■ A hand appears under the icon for the shared folder.

SHARE A PRINTER

You can share your printer with other individuals on a network.

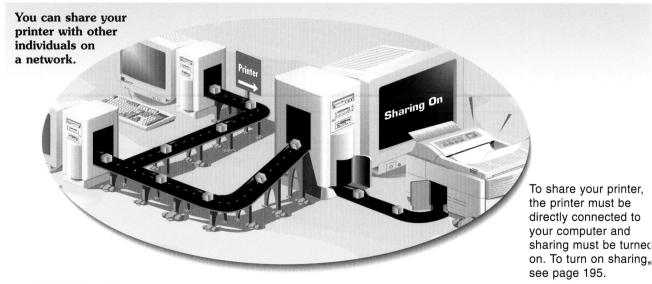

To share your printer, the printer must be directly connected to your computer and sharing must be turned on. To turn on sharing, see page 195.

To turn on sharing, see page 195.

SHARE A PRINTER

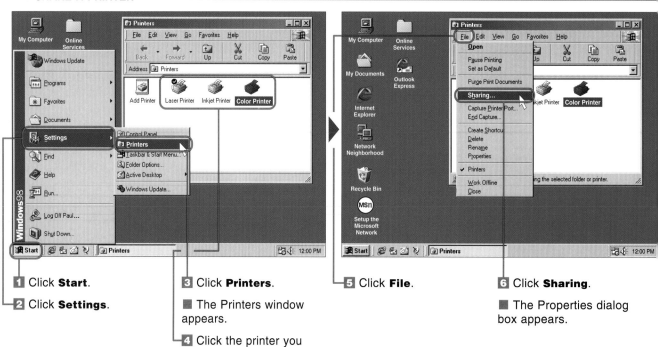

1 Click **Start**.

2 Click **Settings**.

3 Click **Printers**.

■ The Printers window appears.

4 Click the printer you want to share.

5 Click **File**.

6 Click **Sharing**.

■ The Properties dialog box appears.

Will sharing a printer affect my computer's performance?

When individuals on the network send files to your printer, your computer temporarily stores the files before sending them to the printer. As a result, your computer will operate more slowly while other people are using your printer.

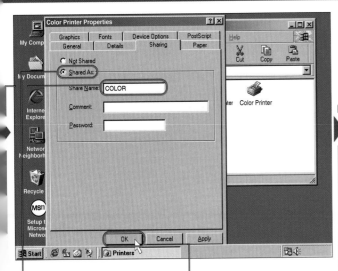

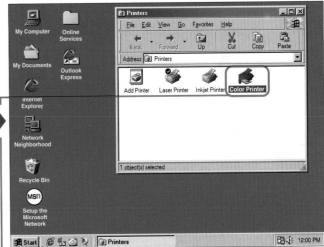

7 Click **Shared As:** (○ changes to ⊙).

■ This area displays the name of the printer people will see on the network.

8 Click **OK** to confirm your change.

■ Your printer is now available to other people on the network.

■ A hand appears under the icon for the printer you have shared.

Note: To use your printer, your colleagues must install the printer software on their computers. To install printer software, see page 182.

■ To turn off printer sharing, repeat steps **1** to **8**, selecting **Not Shared** in step **7**.

BROWSE THROUGH A NETWORK

You can easily browse through the information available on your network.

A network consists of one or more groups of computers, called workgroups. The computers in a workgroup frequently share resources, such as a printer.

BROWSE THROUGH A NETWORK

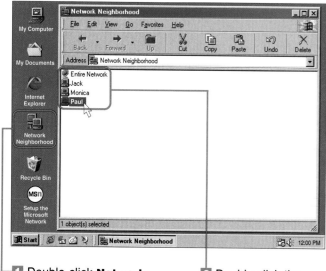

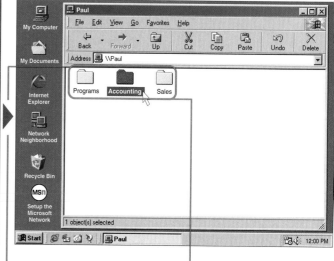

1 Double-click **Network Neighborhood**.

■ The Network Neighborhood window appears. The window displays all the computers in your workgroup.

2 Double-click the computer containing the files with which you want to work.

Note: You can double-click **Entire Network** *to view other computers on the network that are not in your workgroup.*

■ The folders shared by the computer appears.

3 Double-click the folder containing the files with which you want to work.

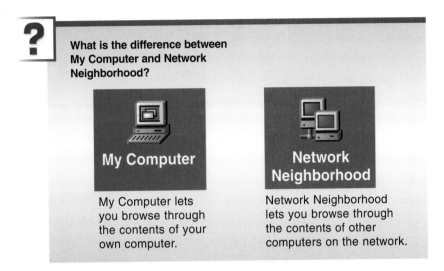

What is the difference between My Computer and Network Neighborhood?

My Computer

My Computer lets you browse through the contents of your own computer.

Network Neighborhood

Network Neighborhood lets you browse through the contents of other computers on the network.

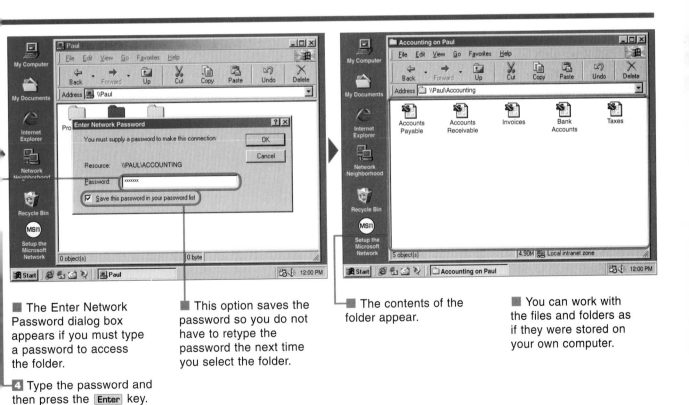

■ The Enter Network Password dialog box appears if you must type a password to access the folder.

■ This option saves the password so you do not have to retype the password the next time you select the folder.

■ The contents of the folder appear.

■ You can work with the files and folders as if they were stored on your own computer.

4 Type the password and then press the Enter key.

CHANGE THE DEFAULT PRINTER

If you have access to more than one printer, you can choose which printer you want to automatically print your documents.

CHANGE THE DEFAULT PRINTER

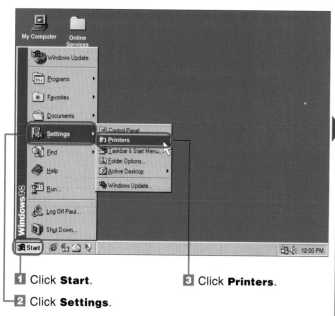

1 Click **Start**.

2 Click **Settings**.

3 Click **Printers**.

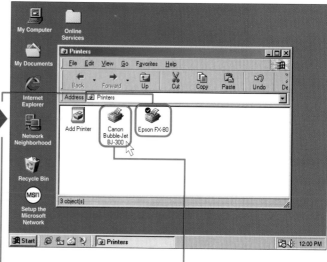

■ The Printers window appears. The window displays the printers you can use to print your documents.

■ The default printer displays a check mark (✓).

4 Click the printer you want to set as your new default printer.

?

Which printer should I select as my default printer?

When selecting a default printer, you should choose the printer you use most often. The printer you select should also be close to your desk and offer the capabilities you need.

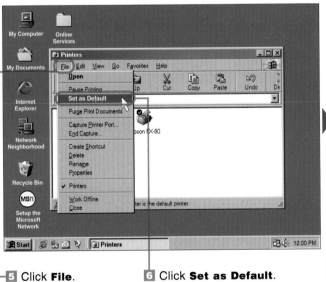

-5 Click **File**.

-6 Click **Set as Default**.

■ The new default printer displays a check mark (✔).

■ Your documents will automatically print to the new default printer.

-7 Click ✗ to close the Printers window.

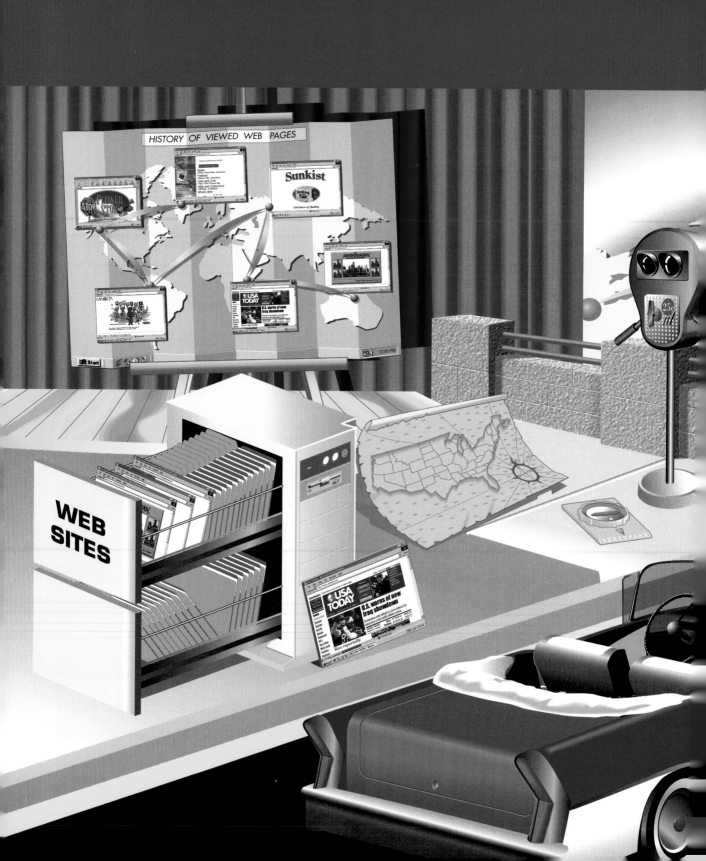

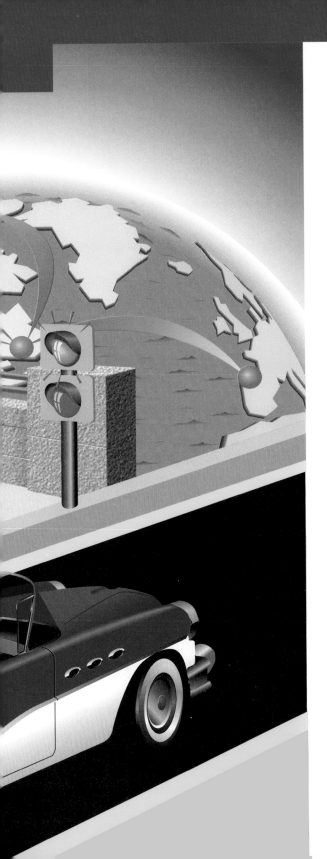

CHAPTER 10

Browse the Web

This chapter will explain how the Web works and how you can use it to transfer information from sites around the world.

INTRODUCTION TO THE WEB

The World Wide Web is part of the Internet, which is the largest computer system in the world. The Web consists of a huge collection of documents stored on hundreds of thousands of computers.

Web Pages

A Web page is a document on the Web. You can find Web pages on every subject imaginable. There are Web pages that offer information such as newspaper and magazine articles, movie clips, recipes, Shakespearean plays, airline schedules and more. You can also purchase items, do your banking and get programs and games on the Web.

Web Sites

A Web site is a collection of Web pages maintained by a college, university, government agency, company or individual.

URLs

Each Web page has a unique address, called a Uniform Resource Locator (URL). You can display any Web page if you know its URL.

Most Web page URLs start with http (HyperText Transfer Protocol).

Links

Web pages contain highlighted text or images, called links, that connect to other pages on the Web. You can select a link on a Web page to display another page located on the same computer or a computer across the city, country or world.

Links allow you to easily move through a vast amount of information by jumping from one Web page to another. This is known as "browsing the Web."

Connecting to the Internet

Most people use an Internet Service Provider (ISP) to connect to the Internet. Once you pay your service provider to connect to the Internet, you can exchange information on the Internet free of charge.

START INTERNET EXPLORER

You can start Internet Explorer to browse through the information on the Web.

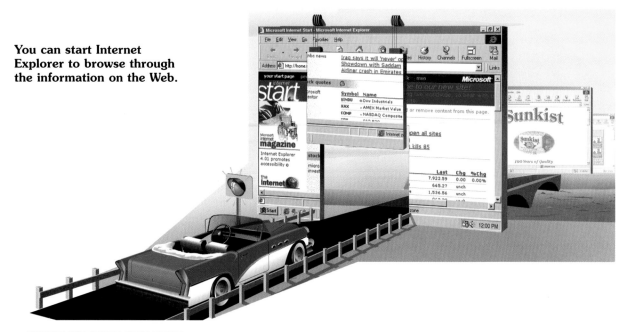

START INTERNET EXPLORER

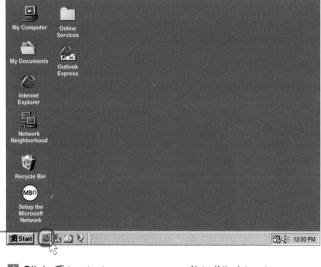

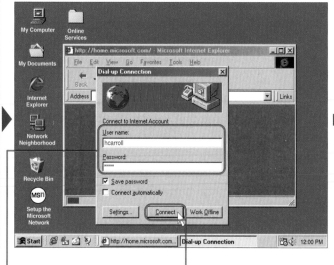

1 Click 🅔 to start Internet Explorer and begin browsing the Web.

Note: If the Internet Connection Wizard appears, see the top of page 213.

■ The Dial-up Connection dialog box appears.

■ This area displays your user name and password.

Note: An asterisk (*) appears for each character in your password to prevent others from viewing the password.

2 Click **Connect** to connect to your Internet service provider.

? Why does the Internet Connection Wizard appear when I try to start Internet Explorer?

The Internet Connection Wizard appears the first time you start Internet Explorer to help you get connected to the Internet. You can use the wizard to set up a new connection to the Internet or to set up an existing account. To set up an existing account, ask your Internet service provider for the information you need to enter.

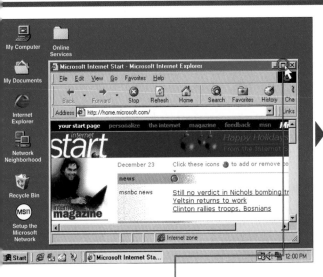

■ The Microsoft Internet Explorer window appears, displaying the Internet Start Web page.

Note: A different Web page may appear on your screen.

3 Click 🔲 to maximize the window to fill your screen.

■ The window maximizes to fill your screen.

DISPLAY A SPECIFIC WEB PAGE

You can easily display a page on the Web that you have heard or read about.

You need to know the address of the Web page you want to view. Each page on the Web has a unique address, called a Uniform Resource Locator (URL).

■ DISPLAY A SPECIFIC WEB PAGE

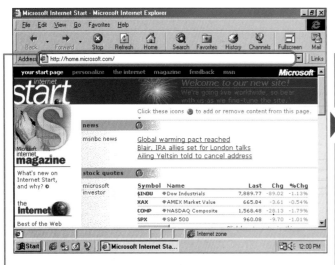

1 Click this area to highlight the current Web page address.

2 Type the address of the Web page you want to view and then press the **Enter** key.

■ When you start typing the address of a Web page you have previously typed, Internet Explorer completes the address for you.

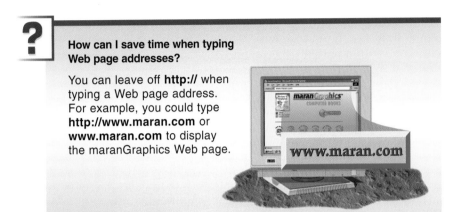

How can I save time when typing Web page addresses?

You can leave off **http://** when typing a Web page address. For example, you could type **http://www.maran.com** or **www.maran.com** to display the maranGraphics Web page.

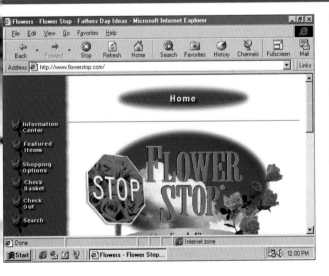

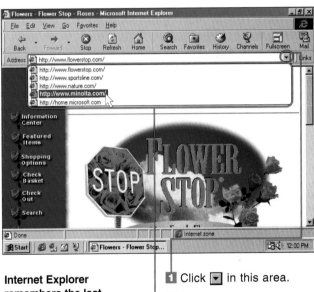

■ The Web page appears on your screen.

Internet Explorer remembers the last Web page addresses you typed. You can select one of these addresses to quickly display a Web page.

■1 Click ▼ in this area.

■2 Click the address of the Web page you want to display.

SELECT A LINK

A link connects text or a picture on one Web page to another Web page. When you select the text or picture, the other Web page appears.

■ SELECT A LINK ■

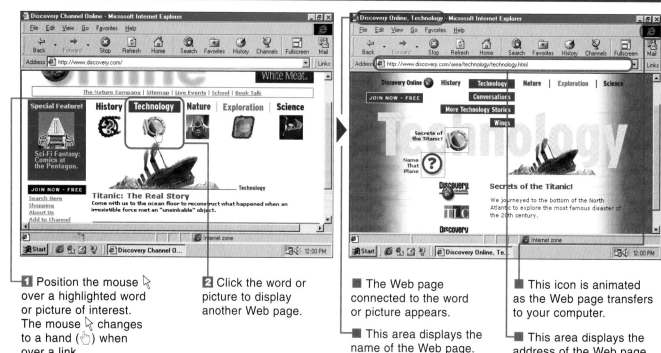

1 Position the mouse ⬚ over a highlighted word or picture of interest. The mouse ⬚ changes to a hand (🖑) when over a link.

2 Click the word or picture to display another Web page.

■ The Web page connected to the word or picture appears.

■ This area displays the name of the Web page.

■ This icon is animated as the Web page transfers to your computer.

■ This area displays the address of the Web page.

REFRESH A WEB PAGE

You can refresh a Web page to update the displayed information, such as the current news. Internet Explorer will transfer a fresh copy of the Web page to your computer.

REFRESH A WEB PAGE

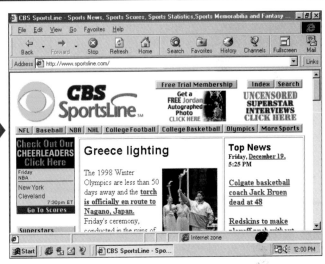

1 Click **Refresh** to transfer a fresh copy of the displayed Web page to your computer.

■ A fresh copy of the Web page appears on your screen.

STOP TRANSFER OF INFORMATION

If a Web page is taking a long time to appear on your screen, you can stop transferring the page and try connecting again later.

The best time to try connecting to a Web site is during off-peak hours, such as nights and weekends, when fewer people are using the Internet.

STOP TRANSFER OF INFORMATION

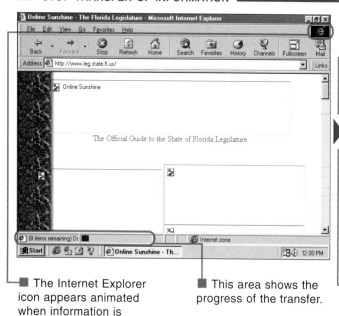

■ The Internet Explorer icon appears animated when information is transferring to your computer.

■ This area shows the progress of the transfer.

1 Click **Stop** to stop the transfer of information.

■ You may also want to stop the transfer of information if you realize a Web page is of no interest to you.

You can easily move back
and forth through Web
pages you have viewed
since you last started
Internet Explorer.

MOVE THROUGH WEB PAGES

-◻1 Click **Back** to display
the last Web page you
viewed.

◼ Click **Forward** to
move forward through
the Web pages you
have viewed.

**You can display a list of
the Web pages you have
viewed.**

-◻1 Click ▾ beside **Back** or
Forward to display a list
of Web pages you have
viewed. A menu appears.

◻2 Click the Web page
you want to view.

DISPLAY AND CHANGE YOUR HOME PAGE

You can specify which Web page you want to appear each time you start Internet Explorer. This page is called your home page.

DISPLAY AND CHANGE YOUR HOME PAGE

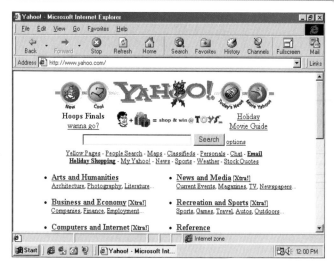

DISPLAY YOUR HOME PAGE

1 Click **Home** to display your home page.

■ Internet Explorer initially sets the Microsoft Internet Start page as your home page.

Note: Your home page may be different.

CHANGE YOUR HOME PAGE

1 Display the Web page you want to set as your home page.

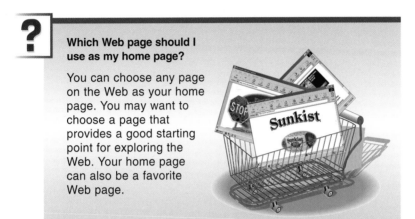

Which Web page should I use as my home page?

You can choose any page on the Web as your home page. You may want to choose a page that provides a good starting point for exploring the Web. Your home page can also be a favorite Web page.

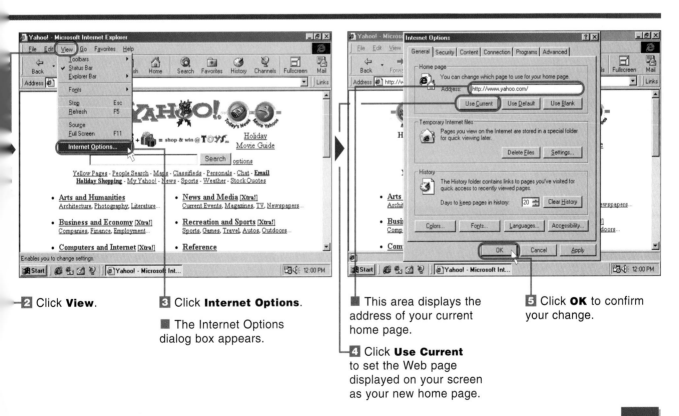

2 Click **View**.

3 Click **Internet Options**.

■ The Internet Options dialog box appears.

■ This area displays the address of your current home page.

4 Click **Use Current** to set the Web page displayed on your screen as your new home page.

5 Click **OK** to confirm your change.

ADD A WEB PAGE TO FAVORITES

You can use the Favorites feature to create a list of Web pages you frequently visit. You can quickly return to any Web page in the list.

ADD A WEB PAGE TO FAVORITES

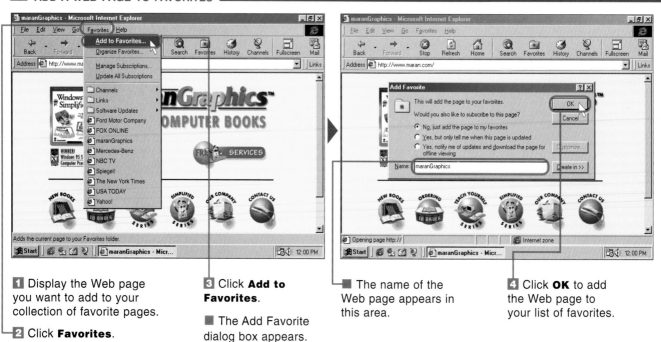

1 Display the Web page you want to add to your collection of favorite pages.

2 Click **Favorites**.

3 Click **Add to Favorites**.

■ The Add Favorite dialog box appears.

■ The name of the Web page appears in this area.

4 Click **OK** to add the Web page to your list of favorites.

What are the benefits of adding a Web page to my list of favorites?

Web page addresses can be long and complex. Selecting Web pages from your list of favorites saves you from having to remember and constantly retype the same addresses over and over again.

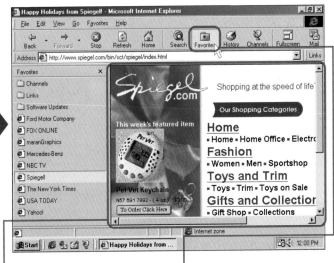

VIEW A FAVORITE WEB PAGE

1 Click **Favorites** to display a list of your favorite Web pages.

■ A list of your favorite Web pages appears in this area.

2 Click the favorite Web page you want to view.

Note: To display the favorite Web pages in a folder, click the folder ( ).

■ The favorite Web page you selected appears in this area.

■ You can repeat step **2** to view another favorite Web page.

3 When you finish viewing your list of favorite Web pages, click **Favorites** to hide the list.

DISPLAY HISTORY OF VIEWED WEB PAGES

Internet Explorer keeps track of the Web pages you have recently viewed. You can easily return to any of these pages.

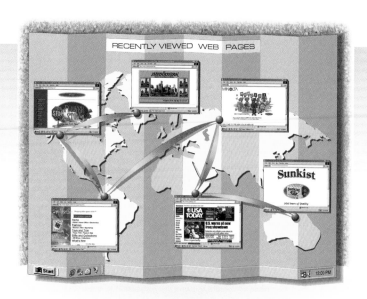

DISPLAY HISTORY OF VIEWED WEB PAGES

1 Click **History** to display a list of the Web pages you have recently viewed.

■ A history of Web pages you have recently viewed appears in this area.

2 Click the week or day you viewed the Web page you want to view again. The 🔲 symbol appears beside each week and day.

■ The Web sites you viewed during the week or day appear. The 🔲 symbol appears beside each Web site.

3 Click the Web site of interest.

How long does Internet Explorer keep track of the Web pages I have viewed?

Internet Explorer keeps track of the Web pages you have viewed during the last 20 days.

■ The Web pages you viewed at the Web site appear. The 🔲 symbol appears beside each Web page.

4 Click the Web page you want to view.

■ The Web page appears in this area.

■ You can repeat step **4** to view another Web page.

5 When you have finished working with your list of recently viewed Web pages, click **History** to hide the list.

SEARCH THE WEB

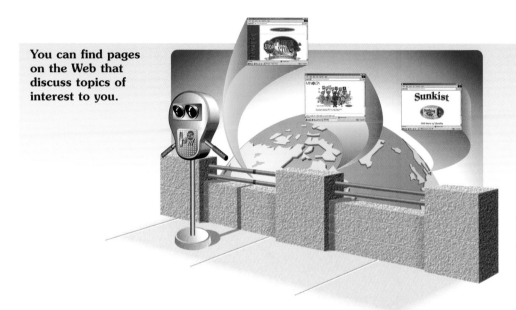

You can find pages on the Web that discuss topics of interest to you.

There are search tools available on the Web that catalog information about millions of Web pages. Popular search tools include Excite, Lycos and Yahoo!

■■ SEARCH THE WEB ■■■■■■■■

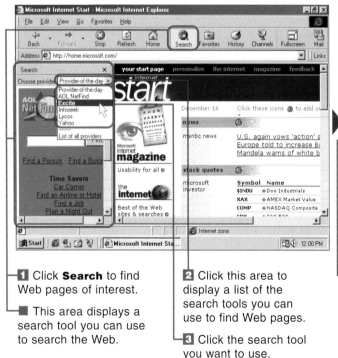

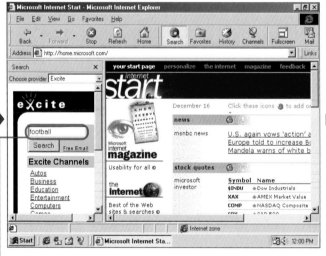

1 Click **Search** to find Web pages of interest.

■ This area displays a search tool you can use to search the Web.

2 Click this area to display a list of the search tools you can use to find Web pages.

3 Click the search tool you want to use.

4 Click this area and then type a word you want to search for.

5 Press the Enter key to start the search.

How do search tools find Web pages?

Some search tools use a program, called a robot, to scan the Web for new and updated pages. Thousands of new Web pages are located and cataloged by robots every day. New pages are also cataloged when people submit information about the pages they have created.

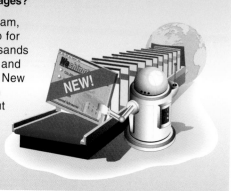

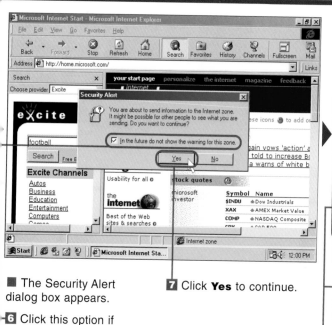

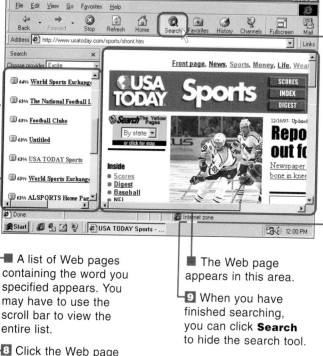

■ The Security Alert dialog box appears.

6 Click this option if you do not want to see this warning again (☐ changes to ☑).

7 Click **Yes** to continue.

■ A list of Web pages containing the word you specified appears. You may have to use the scroll bar to view the entire list.

8 Click the Web page you want to view.

■ The Web page appears in this area.

9 When you have finished searching, you can click **Search** to hide the search tool.

CHAPTER 11

Exchange Electronic Mail

E-mail is a fast, economical way to send messages to people around the world. This chapter will show you how to work with your e-mail, including how to read, send, reply to and forward messages.

INTRODUCTION TO E-MAIL

You can exchange electronic mail (e-mail) with people around the world.

E-mail provides a fast, economical and convenient way to send messages to family, friends and colleagues.

Cost

Once you pay a service provider for a connection to the Internet, there is no charge for sending and receiving e-mail. You do not have to pay extra if you send a long message or if the message travels around the world.

Exchanging e-mail can save you money on long-distance calls. The next time you are about to pick up the telephone, consider sending an e-mail message instead.

Convenience

You can create and send e-mail messages at any time. Unlike telephone calls, the person receiving the message does not have to be at the computer when you send the message. E-mail makes communicating with people in different time zones very convenient.

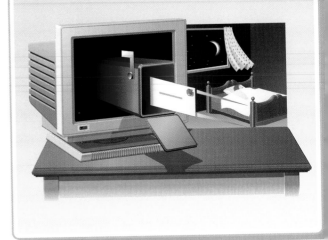

Parts of an E-mail Address

You can send a message to anyone around the world if you know the person's e-mail address. An e-mail address defines the location of an individual's mailbox on the Internet.

An e-mail address consists of two parts separated by the @ ("at") symbol. An e-mail address cannot contain spaces.

mvickers@sales.abc.com

■ The **user name** is the name of the person's account. This can be a real name or a nickname.

■ The **domain name** is the location of the person's account on the Internet. Periods (.) separate the various parts of the domain name.

COMPOSING AN E-MAIL MESSAGE

Smileys

You can use special characters, called smileys or emoticons, to express emotions in e-mail messages. These characters resemble human faces if you turn them sideways.

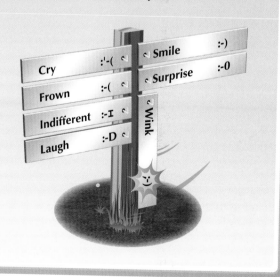

Cry	:'-(
Frown	:-(
Indifferent	:-I
Laugh	:-D
Smile	:-)
Surprise	:-0
Wink	;-)

Shouting

A MESSAGE WRITTEN IN CAPITAL LETTERS IS ANNOYING AND HARD TO READ. THIS IS CALLED SHOUTING. Always use upper and lower case letters when typing e-mail messages.

HOW ARE YOU?

START OUTLOOK EXPRESS

You can start Outlook Express to exchange e-mail messages with people around the world.

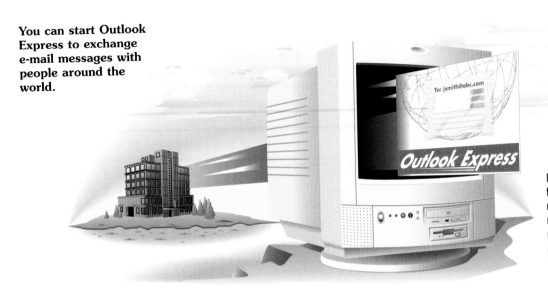

E-mail travels much faster than regular mail, called "snail mail". An e-mail message can travel around the world in minutes.

START OUTLOOK EXPRESS

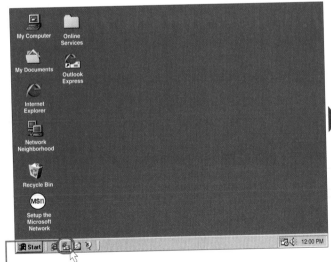

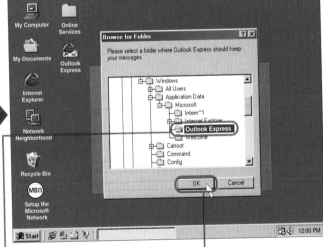

◼︎1 Click 🖥 to start Outlook Express.

Note: If the Internet Connection Wizard appears, see the top of page 213.

◼︎ The Browse for Folder dialog box appears the first time you start Outlook Express.

◼︎ Outlook Express will keep your messages in the highlighted folder.

◼︎2 Click **OK** to keep your messages in the highlighted folder.

Can I use Outlook Express to e-mail famous people?

You can send a message to anyone if you know the e-mail address. Here are some famous e-mail addresses.

NAME	ADDRESS
Bill Gates	askbill@microsoft.com
Brad Pitt	CIAOBOX@MSN.com
James Woods	jameswoods@aol.com
President	president@whitehouse.gov
Tom Brokaw	nightly@nbc.com
Tom Clancy	tomclancy@aol.com

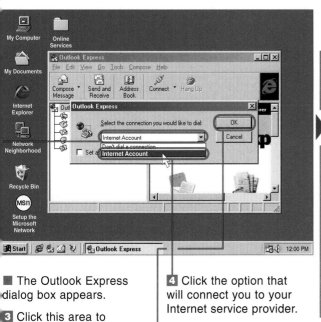

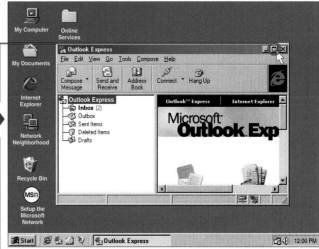

■ The Outlook Express dialog box appears.

3 Click this area to display a list of the dial-up connections set up on your computer.

4 Click the option that will connect you to your Internet service provider.

5 Click **OK** to connect to your Internet service provider.

■ The Outlook Express window appears.

6 Click ▣ to maximize the Outlook Express window to fill your screen.

■ The window maximizes to fill your screen.

READ MESSAGES

You can easily open
your messages to
read their contents.

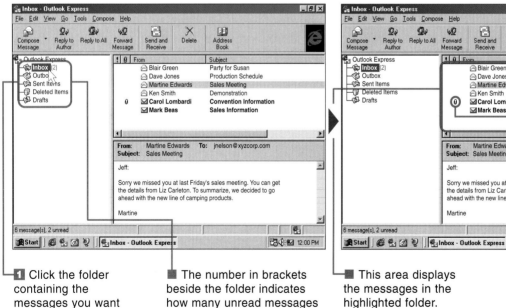

Chris,
The drafts for the advertising
campaign are ready. Will you
be free at 2:00 p.m. tomorrow
to discuss them?

Henry

READ MESSAGES

■**1** Click the folder
containing the
messages you want
to read. The folder
is highlighted.

■ The number in brackets
beside the folder indicates
how many unread messages
the folder contains. The
number disappears when
you have read all the
messages in the folder.

■ This area displays
the messages in the
highlighted folder.
Messages you have not
read display a closed
envelope (✉) and
appear in **bold** type.

■ A paper clip icon (📎)
appears beside a message
with an attached file.

234

?

What folders does Outlook Express use to store my messages?

Inbox
Stores messages sent to you.

Outbox
Temporarily stores messages that have not yet been sent.

Sent Items
Stores copies of messages you have sent.

Deleted Items
Stores messages you have deleted.

Drafts
Stores messages you have not yet completed.

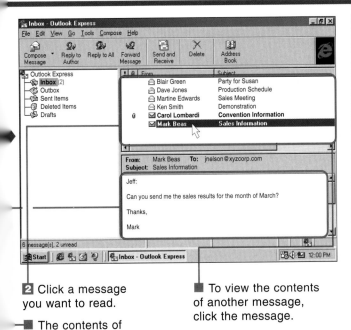

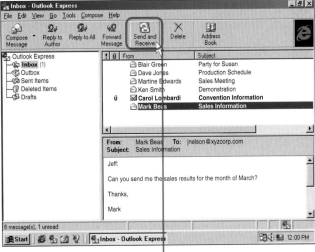

■2 Click a message you want to read.

■ The contents of the message appear in this area.

■ To view the contents of another message, click the message.

GET NEW MESSAGES

Outlook Express automatically checks for new messages every 30 minutes.

■1 To immediately check for new messages, click **Send and Receive**.

COMPOSE A MESSAGE

You can send a message to exchange ideas or request information.

COMPOSE A MESSAGE

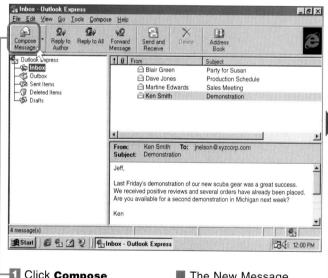

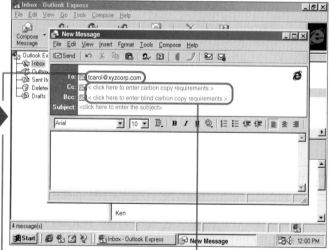

1 Click **Compose Message**.

■ The New Message window appears.

2 Type the e-mail address of the person you want to receive the message.

Note: To select a name from the address book, see page 240. Then skip to step 4.

3 To send a copy of the message to another person, click one of these areas and then type the e-mail address.

Note: For information on sending copies, see the top of page 241.

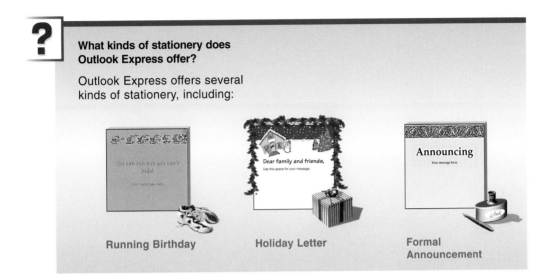

What kinds of stationery does Outlook Express offer?

Outlook Express offers several kinds of stationery, including:

Running Birthday   Holiday Letter   Formal Announcement

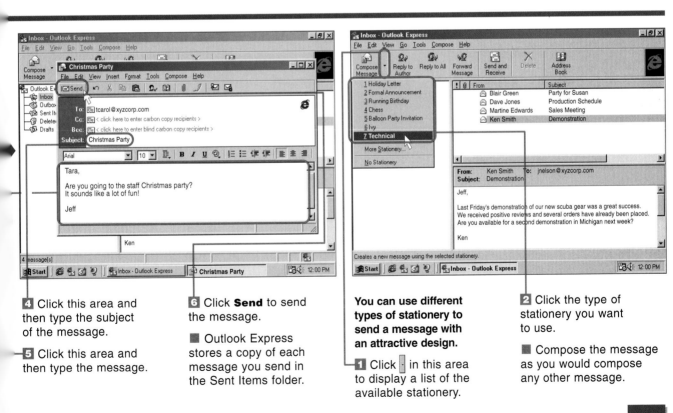

■4 Click this area and then type the subject of the message.

■5 Click this area and then type the message.

■6 Click **Send** to send the message.

■ Outlook Express stores a copy of each message you send in the Sent Items folder.

You can use different types of stationery to send a message with an attractive design.

■1 Click · in this area to display a list of the available stationery.

■2 Click the type of stationery you want to use.

■ Compose the message as you would compose any other message.

ADD A NAME TO THE ADDRESS BOOK

You can use the address book to store the e-mail addresses of people to whom you frequently send messages.

ADD A NAME TO THE ADDRESS BOOK

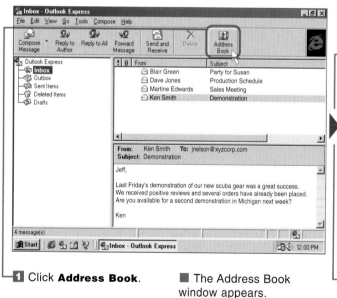

1 Click **Address Book**.

■ The Address Book window appears.

2 Click **New Contact** to add a name to the address book.

■ The Properties dialog box appears.

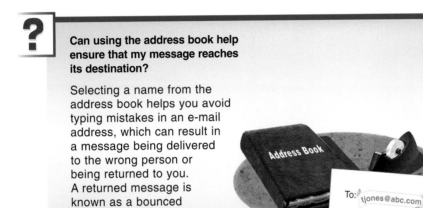

? **Can using the address book help ensure that my message reaches its destination?**

Selecting a name from the address book helps you avoid typing mistakes in an e-mail address, which can result in a message being delivered to the wrong person or being returned to you. A returned message is known as a bounced message.

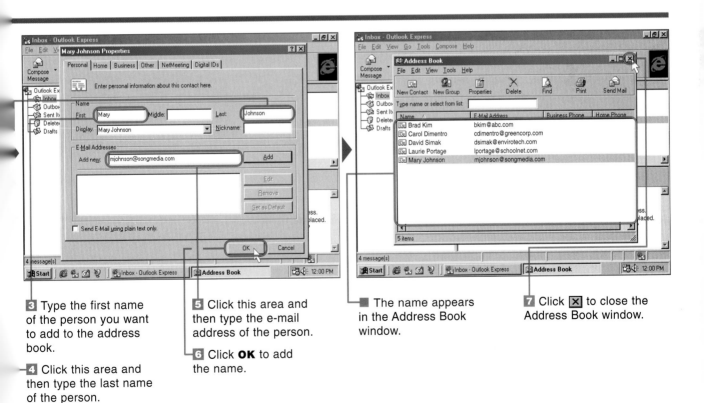

3 Type the first name of the person you want to add to the address book.

4 Click this area and then type the last name of the person.

5 Click this area and then type the e-mail address of the person.

6 Click **OK** to add the name.

■ The name appears in the Address Book window.

7 Click ☒ to close the Address Book window.

SELECT A NAME FROM THE ADDRESS BOOK

When sending a message, you can select the name of the person you want to receive the message from the address book.

Selecting names from the address book saves you from having to remember e-mail addresses you often use.

■ SELECT A NAME FROM THE ADDRESS BOOK ■

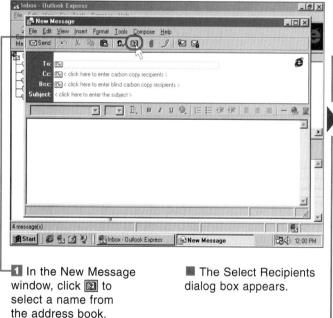

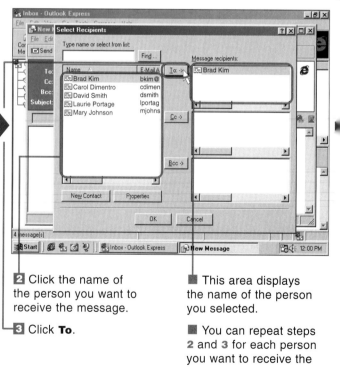

1 In the New Message window, click 🔲 to select a name from the address book.

Note: To display the New Message window, perform step 1 on page 236.

■ The Select Recipients dialog box appears.

2 Click the name of the person you want to receive the message.

3 Click **To**.

■ This area displays the name of the person you selected.

■ You can repeat steps **2** and **3** for each person you want to receive the message.

240

? **How can I address a message I want to send?**

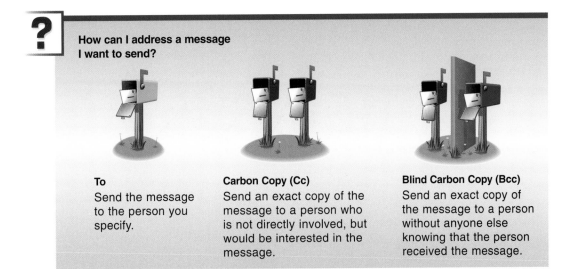

To
Send the message to the person you specify.

Carbon Copy (Cc)
Send an exact copy of the message to a person who is not directly involved, but would be interested in the message.

Blind Carbon Copy (Bcc)
Send an exact copy of the message to a person without anyone else knowing that the person received the message.

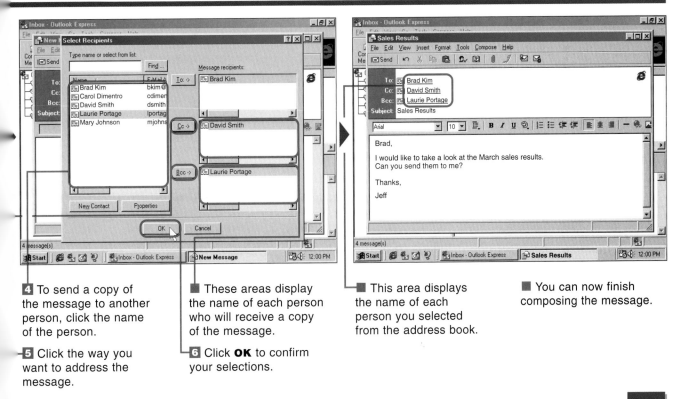

■4 To send a copy of the message to another person, click the name of the person.

■ These areas display the name of each person who will receive a copy of the message.

■ This area displays the name of each person you selected from the address book.

■ You can now finish composing the message.

■5 Click the way you want to address the message.

■6 Click **OK** to confirm your selections.

ATTACH A FILE TO A MESSAGE

You can attach a file to a
message you are sending.
Attaching a file is useful
when you want to include
additional information
with a message.

ATTACH A FILE TO A MESSAGE

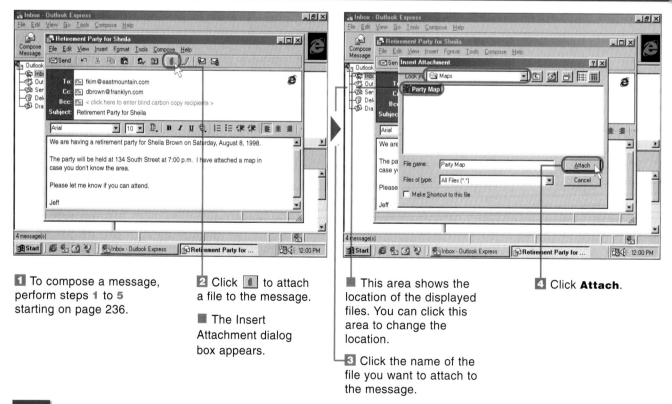

1 To compose a message,
perform steps **1** to **5**
starting on page 236.

2 Click 📎 to attach
a file to the message.

■ The Insert
Attachment dialog
box appears.

■ This area shows the
location of the displayed
files. You can click this
area to change the
location.

3 Click the name of the
file you want to attach to
the message.

4 Click **Attach**.

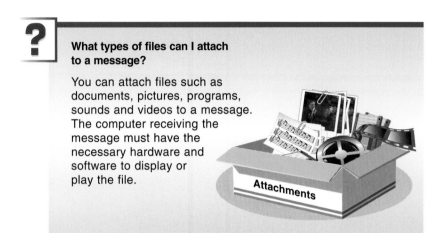

What types of files can I attach to a message?

You can attach files such as documents, pictures, programs, sounds and videos to a message. The computer receiving the message must have the necessary hardware and software to display or play the file.

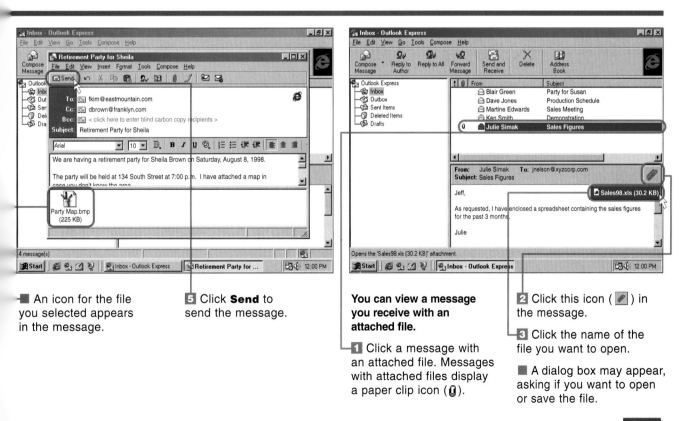

◀■ An icon for the file you selected appears in the message.

5 Click **Send** to send the message.

You can view a message you receive with an attached file.

1 Click a message with an attached file. Messages with attached files display a paper clip icon (📎).

2 Click this icon (📎) in the message.

3 Click the name of the file you want to open.

■ A dialog box may appear, asking if you want to open or save the file.

REPLY TO A MESSAGE

You can reply to a message to answer a question or comment on the message.

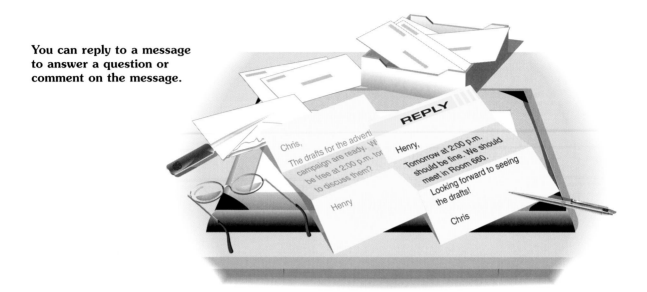

REPLY TO A MESSAGE

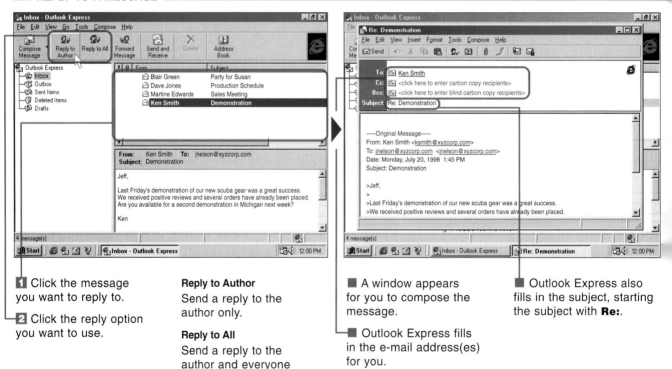

1 Click the message you want to reply to.

2 Click the reply option you want to use.

Reply to Author

Send a reply to the author only.

Reply to All

Send a reply to the author and everyone who received the original message.

■ A window appears for you to compose the message.

■ Outlook Express fills in the e-mail address(es) for you.

■ Outlook Express also fills in the subject, starting the subject with **Re:**.

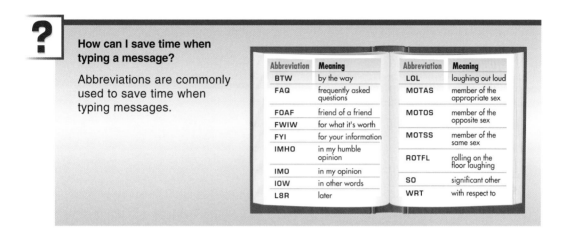

How can I save time when typing a message?

Abbreviations are commonly used to save time when typing messages.

Abbreviation	Meaning
BTW	by the way
FAQ	frequently asked questions
FOAF	friend of a friend
FWIW	for what it's worth
FYI	for your information
IMHO	in my humble opinion
IMO	in my opinion
IOW	in other words
L8R	later

Abbreviation	Meaning
LOL	laughing out loud
MOTAS	member of the appropriate sex
MOTOS	member of the opposite sex
MOTSS	member of the same sex
ROTFL	rolling on the floor laughing
SO	significant other
WRT	with respect to

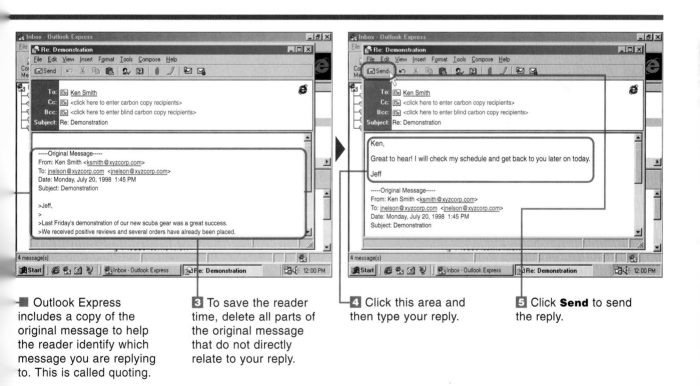

■ Outlook Express includes a copy of the original message to help the reader identify which message you are replying to. This is called quoting.

3 To save the reader time, delete all parts of the original message that do not directly relate to your reply.

4 Click this area and then type your reply.

5 Click **Send** to send the reply.

FORWARD A MESSAGE

After reading a message, you can add comments and then forward the message to a friend or colleague.

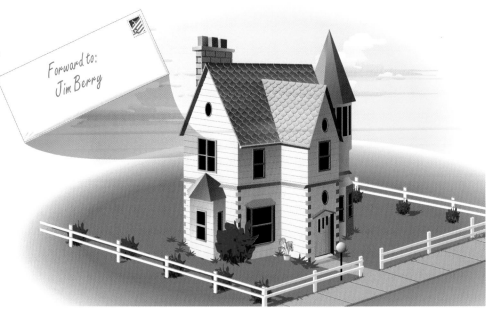

FORWARD A MESSAGE

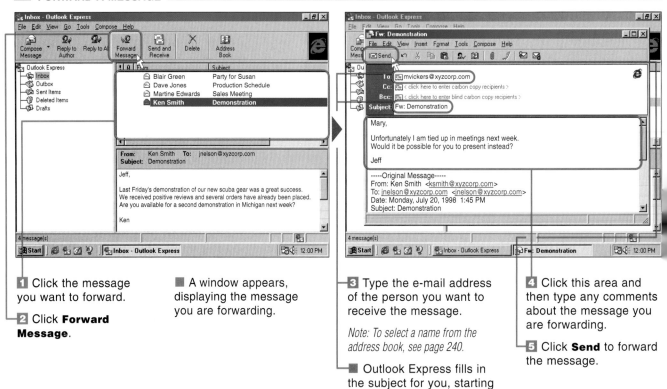

1 Click the message you want to forward.

2 Click **Forward Message**.

■ A window appears, displaying the message you are forwarding.

3 Type the e-mail address of the person you want to receive the message.

Note: To select a name from the address book, see page 240.

■ Outlook Express fills in the subject for you, starting the subject with **Fw:**.

4 Click this area and then type any comments about the message you are forwarding.

5 Click **Send** to forward the message.

You can delete a message you no longer need. Deleting messages prevents your folders from becoming cluttered with messages.

DELETE A MESSAGE

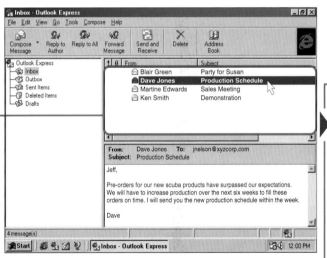

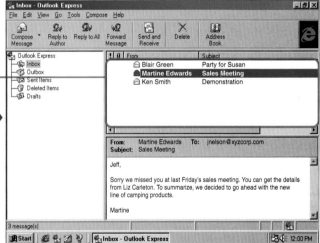

■1 Click the message you want to delete.

■2 Press the Delete key.

■ Outlook Express removes the message from the current folder and places the message in the Deleted Items folder.

Note: Deleting a message from the Deleted Items folder will permanently remove the message from your computer.

ADD A SIGNATURE TO MESSAGES

You can have Outlook Express add information about yourself to the end of every message you send. A signature saves you from having to type the same information every time you send a message.

ADD A SIGNATURE TO MESSAGES

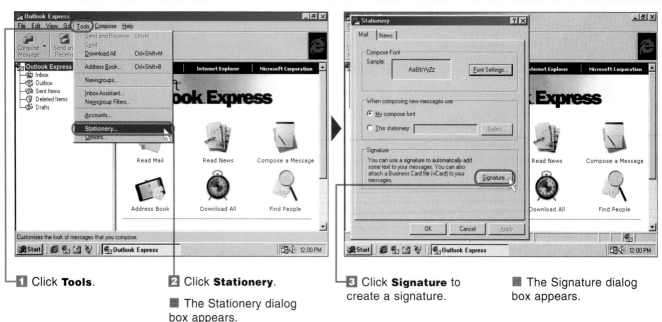

1 Click **Tools**.

2 Click **Stationery**.

■ The Stationery dialog box appears.

3 Click **Signature** to create a signature.

■ The Signature dialog box appears.

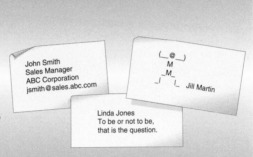

What can I include in a signature?

A signature can include information such as your name, e-mail address, occupation, favorite quotation or Web page address. You can also use plain characters to display simple pictures. As a courtesy to people who will read your messages, do not create a signature that is more than four lines long.

John Smith
Sales Manager
ABC Corporation
jsmith@sales.abc.com

(_@_)
M
_M_
_I_ _L_ Jill Martin

Linda Jones
To be or not to be,
that is the question.

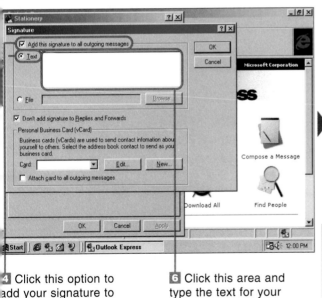

4 Click this option to add your signature to the messages you send (☐ changes to ☑).

5 Click this option to be able to type the text for your signature (○ changes to ⊙).

6 Click this area and type the text for your signature.

7 Click **OK** to confirm your changes.

8 Click **OK** to close the Stationery dialog box.

■ If you no longer want to add a signature to the messages you send, perform steps **1** to **4** (☑ changes to ☐ in step **4**). Then perform steps **7** and **8**.

CHAPTER 12

Using Newsgroups

Using newsgroups is a great way to communicate with people from different parts of the world. In this chapter you will learn how to subscribe to newsgroups, read messages and much more.

INTRODUCTION TO NEWSGROUPS

A newsgroup is a discussion group that allows people with common interests to communicate with each other.

There are thousands of newsgroups on every subject imaginable. Each newsgroup discusses a particular topic, such as jobs offered, puzzles or medicine.

Newsgroup Names

The name of a newsgroup describes the type of information discussed in the newsgroup. A newsgroup name consists of two or more words, separated by dots (.).

The first word describes the main topic or category (example: **rec** for recreation). Each of the following words narrows the topic.

News Servers

A news server is a computer that stores newsgroup messages. Most news servers are maintained by service providers, which are companies that give you access to the Internet.

After a few days or weeks, newsgroup messages are removed from a news server to make room for new messages.

MAIN NEWSGROUP CATEGORIES

alt (alternative)

General interest discussions that can include unusual and bizarre topics. Some newsgroups include alt.fan.actors, alt.music.alternative and alt.ufo.reports.

biz (business)

Business discussions that are usually more commercial in nature than those in other newsgroups. Some newsgroups include biz.books, biz.jobs.offered and biz.marketplace.services.

comp (computers)

Discussions of computer hardware, software and computer science. Some newsgroups include comp.graphics, comp.security.misc and comp.sys.laptops.

misc (miscellaneous)

Discussions of various topics that may overlap topics discussed in other categories. Some newsgroups include misc.consumers.house, misc.education and misc.forsale.

rec (recreation)

Discussions of recreational activities and hobbies. Some newsgroups include rec.arts.movies.reviews, rec.autos and rec.food.recipes.

sci (science)

Discussions about science, including research, applied science and the social sciences. Some newsgroups include sci.agriculture, sci.energy and sci.physics.

soc (social)

Discussions of social issues, including world cultures and political topics. Some newsgroups include soc.college, soc.history and soc.women.

talk

Debates and long discussions, often about controversial subjects. Some newsgroups include talk.environment, talk.politics and talk.rumors.

SUBSCRIBE TO NEWSGROUPS

You can subscribe to newsgroups you want to read on a regular basis. Outlook Express provides a list of all the available newsgroups so you can find newsgroups of interest.

SUBSCRIBE TO NEWSGROUPS

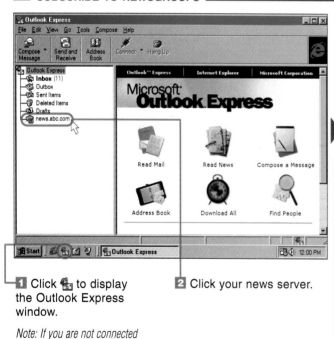

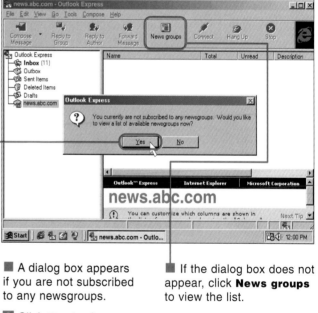

■1 Click 🗐 to display the Outlook Express window.

Note: If you are not connected to the Internet, a dialog box may appear that allows you to connect.

■2 Click your news server.

■ A dialog box appears if you are not subscribed to any newsgroups.

■3 Click **Yes** to view a list of the available newsgroups.

■ If the dialog box does not appear, click **News groups** to view the list.

?

Why is my newsgroup list different from the list shown below?

The newsgroups available to you depend on the news server you use. The available newsgroups may be limited to save valuable storage space on the server.

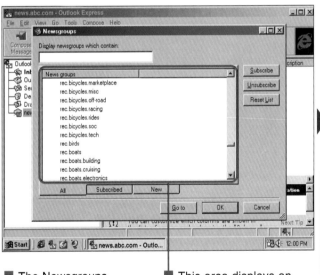

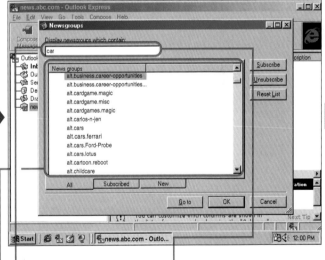

■ The Newsgroups window appears.

■ This area displays an alphabetical list of all the available newsgroups. You can use the scroll bar to browse through the list.

Note: The newsgroup list may take a few minutes to appear the first time you display the list.

4 To find newsgroup names that contain a word of interest, click this area and then type the word.

■ This area displays the newsgroup names that contain the word you typed.

■ To once again display the entire newsgroup list, double-click this area and then press the `Delete` or `◆Backspace` key.

CONTINUED

SUBSCRIBE TO NEWSGROUPS

There are newsgroups on every subject imaginable. You can subscribe to newsgroups on subjects such as football, investments and stamp collecting.

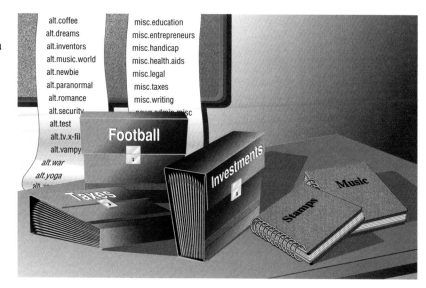

alt.coffee
alt.dreams
alt.inventors
alt.music.world
alt.newbie
alt.paranormal
alt.romance
alt.security
alt.test
alt.tv.x-fil
alt.vampy
alt.war
alt.yoga
alt.z

misc.education
misc.entrepreneurs
misc.handicap
misc.health.aids
misc.legal
misc.taxes
misc.writing
news.admin.misc

SUBSCRIBE TO NEWSGROUPS (CONTINUED)

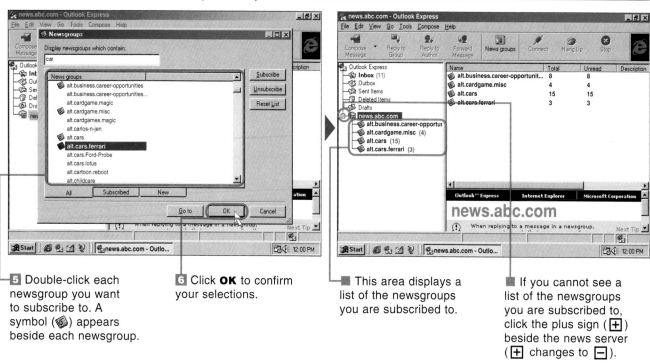

5 Double-click each newsgroup you want to subscribe to. A symbol (🌐) appears beside each newsgroup.

6 Click **OK** to confirm your selections.

■ This area displays a list of the newsgroups you are subscribed to.

■ If you cannot see a list of the newsgroups you are subscribed to, click the plus sign (⊞) beside the news server (⊞ changes to ⊟).

Are there any newsgroups that can help me get started?

The following newsgroups provide useful information for beginners and let you ask questions about newsgroups:

news.answers

news.newusers.questions

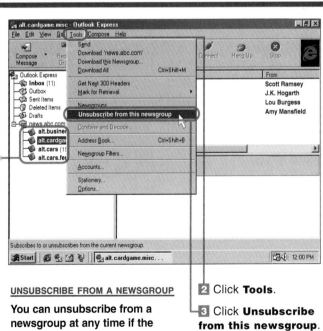

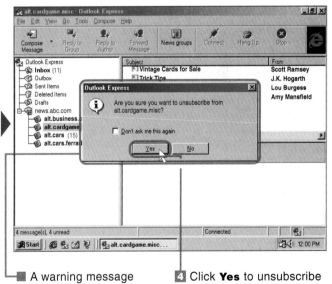

UNSUBSCRIBE FROM A NEWSGROUP

You can unsubscribe from a newsgroup at any time if the subject material no longer interests you.

■1 Click the newsgroup you want to unsubscribe from. The newsgroup is highlighted.

■2 Click **Tools**.

■3 Click **Unsubscribe from this newsgroup**.

■ A warning message appears, asking if you are sure you want to unsubscribe from the newsgroup.

■4 Click **Yes** to unsubscribe from the newsgroup.

■ The newsgroup disappears.

READ MESSAGES

You can read the messages in a newsgroup to learn the opinions and ideas of thousands of people around the world.

READ MESSAGES

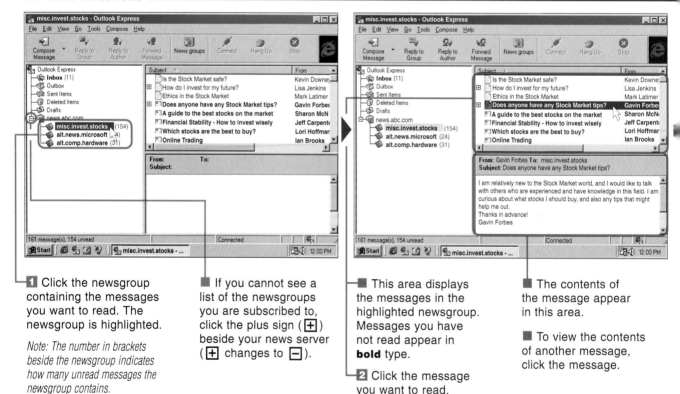

1 Click the newsgroup containing the messages you want to read. The newsgroup is highlighted.

Note: The number in brackets beside the newsgroup indicates how many unread messages the newsgroup contains.

■ If you cannot see a list of the newsgroups you are subscribed to, click the plus sign (⊞) beside your news server (⊞ changes to ⊟).

■ This area displays the messages in the highlighted newsgroup. Messages you have not read appear in **bold** type.

2 Click the message you want to read.

■ The contents of the message appear in this area.

■ To view the contents of another message, click the message.

Where can I find a list of questions that are commonly asked in a newsgroup?

Many newsgroups include a FAQ (Frequently Asked Questions) which is a message containing a list of questions and answers that regularly appear in a newsgroup. The FAQ is designed to prevent new readers from asking questions that have already been answered. The **news.answers** newsgroup provides FAQs for a wide variety of newsgroups.

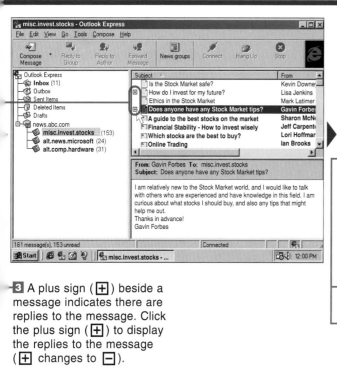

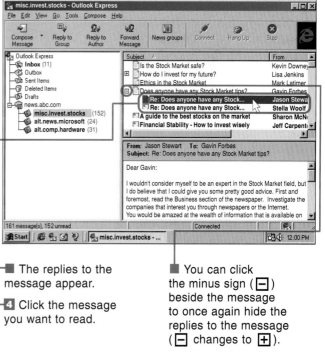

3 A plus sign (⊞) beside a message indicates there are replies to the message. Click the plus sign (⊞) to display the replies to the message (⊞ changes to ⊟).

■ The replies to the message appear.

4 Click the message you want to read.

■ You can click the minus sign (⊟) beside the message to once again hide the replies to the message (⊟ changes to ⊞).

REPLY TO A MESSAGE

You can **reply to** a newsgroup message to answer a question, express an opinion or offer additional information.

Reply to a message only when you have something important to say. A reply such as "Me too" or "I agree" is not very informative.

REPLY TO A MESSAGE

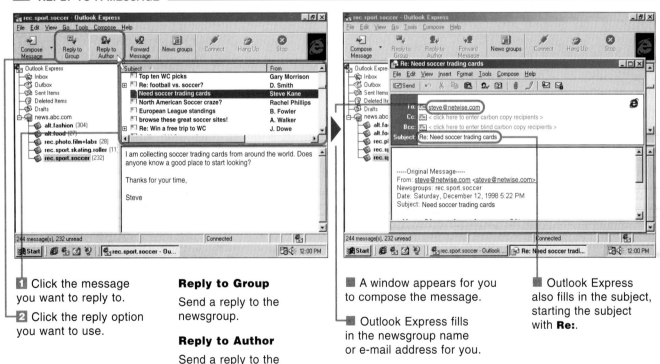

1 Click the message you want to reply to.

2 Click the reply option you want to use.

Reply to Group

Send a reply to the newsgroup.

Reply to Author

Send a reply to the author only.

■ A window appears for you to compose the message.

■ Outlook Express fills in the newsgroup name or e-mail address for you.

■ Outlook Express also fills in the subject, starting the subject with **Re:**.

Who can I send a reply to?

You can send a reply to the newsgroup or just the author of the message. Send a message to just the author when your reply would not be of interest to others in a newsgroup or if you want to send a private response.

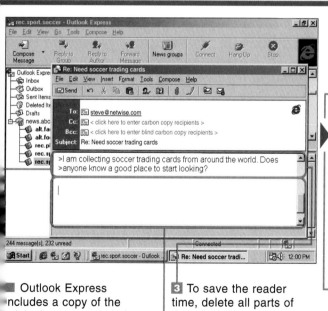

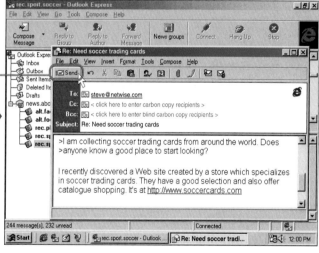

■ Outlook Express includes a copy of the original message to help the reader identify which message you are replying to. This is called quoting. A symbol (>) appears beside each line of quoted text.

3 To save the reader time, delete all parts of the original message that do not directly relate to your reply.

4 Click this area and then type your reply.

5 Click **Post** or **Send** to send your reply.

Note: The appearance of this button depends on the reply option you selected in step 2.

■ A dialog box may appear, stating that your reply was sent to the news server. Click **OK** to close the dialog box.

COMPOSE A MESSAGE

You can send a new message to a newsgroup to ask a question or express an opinion.

When sending a new message to a newsgroup, keep in mind that thousands of people around the world may read the message.

If you want to practice sending a message, send one to the **misc.test** newsgroup. Do not send practice messages to other newsgroups.

■ COMPOSE A MESSAGE ■

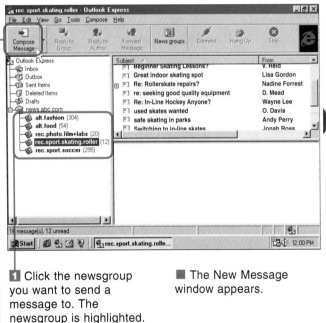

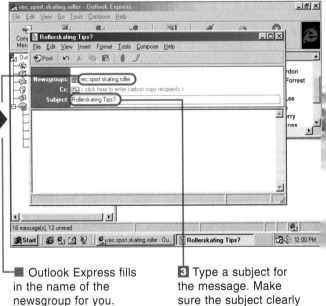

1 Click the newsgroup you want to send a message to. The newsgroup is highlighted.

2 Click **Compose Message**.

■ The New Message window appears.

■ Outlook Express fills in the name of the newsgroup for you.

3 Type a subject for the message. Make sure the subject clearly identifies the contents of your message.

Should I read the messages in a newsgroup before sending a new message?

Reading the messages in a newsgroup without participating is known as lurking. Lurking helps you avoid sending information others have already read and is a great way to learn how people in a newsgroup communicate. You should lurk in a newsgroup for at least one week before sending a new message.

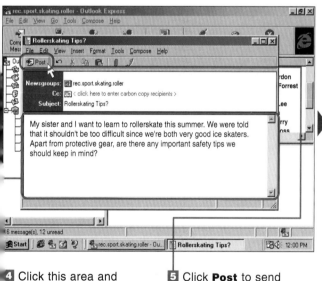

4 Click this area and then type the message. Make sure the message is clear, concise and does not contain spelling or grammar errors.

5 Click **Post** to send the message.

■ A dialog box appears, stating that your message has been sent to the news server.

6 Click **OK** to close the dialog box.

■ Outlook Express stores a copy of each message you send in the Sent Items folder.

CHAPTER 13

Create Web Pages

Find out how to create and edit your own Web pages using FrontPage Express. This chapter shows you how to insert images, create links, publish Web pages and much more.

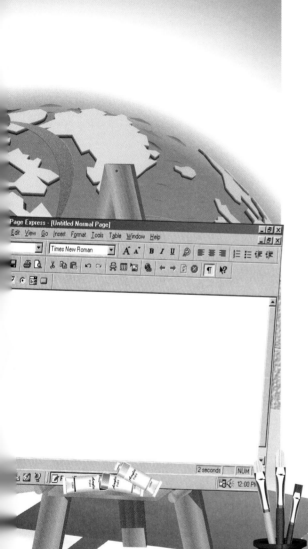

INTRODUCTION TO CREATING WEB PAGES

FrontPage Express allows you to create and edit Web pages. You can place pages you create on the Web so people around the world can view your Web pages.

You can also place Web pages you create on a corporate intranet. An intranet is a small version of the Internet within a company or organization.

■ REASONS FOR PUBLISHING WEB PAGES ■

Personal

Many people use the Web to share information about a topic that interests them. You can create Web pages to discuss your favorite celebrity or hobby, show your favorite pictures, promote a club you belong to or present a résumé to potential employers.

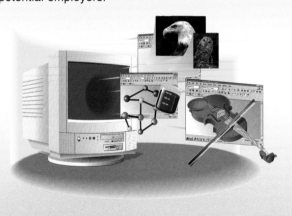

Commercial

Companies use Web pages to keep the public informed about new products, interesting news and job openings within the company. Companies can also allow readers to use their Web pages to place orders for products and services.

START FRONTPAGE EXPRESS

You can start FrontPage Express to create your own Web pages.

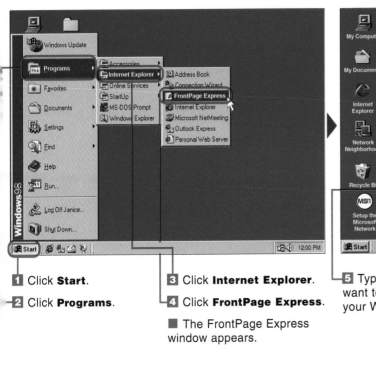

START FRONTPAGE EXPRESS

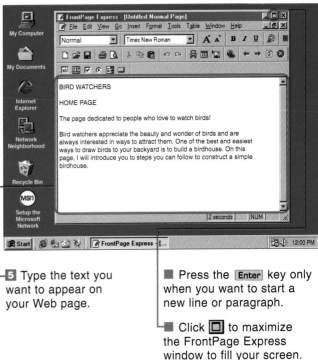

1 Click **Start**.

2 Click **Programs**.

3 Click **Internet Explorer**.

4 Click **FrontPage Express**.

■ The FrontPage Express window appears.

5 Type the text you want to appear on your Web page.

■ Press the Enter key only when you want to start a new line or paragraph.

■ Click □ to maximize the FrontPage Express window to fill your screen.

SAVE A WEB PAGE

You should save a Web
page you create to store
the page for future use.
This lets you later review
and update the Web page.

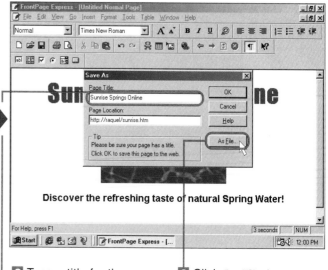

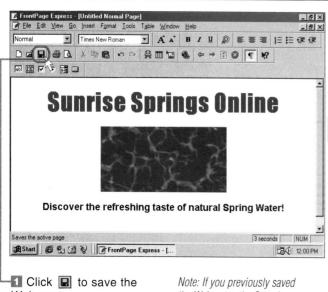

1 Click  to save the
Web page.

■ The Save As dialog
box appears.

*Note: If you previously saved
the Web page, the Save As
dialog box will not appear.*

2 Type a title for the
Web page that describes
the information on the
Web page.

3 Click **As File** to save
the Web page on your
computer.

■ The Save As File
dialog box appears.

268

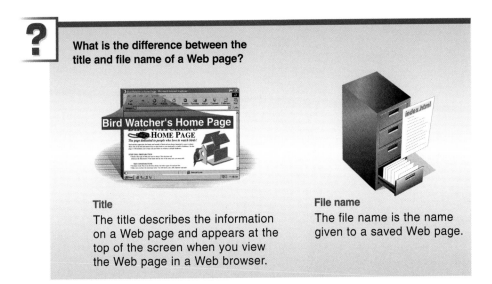

What is the difference between the title and file name of a Web page?

Title

The title describes the information on a Web page and appears at the top of the screen when you view the Web page in a Web browser.

File name

The file name is the name given to a saved Web page.

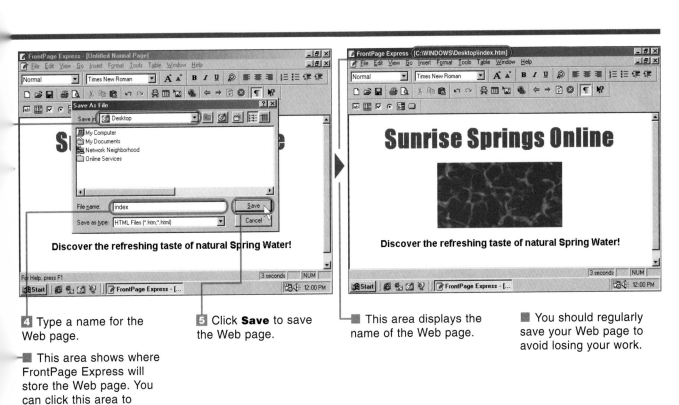

■4 Type a name for the Web page.

─■ This area shows where FrontPage Express will store the Web page. You can click this area to change the location.

■5 Click **Save** to save the Web page.

─■ This area displays the name of the Web page.

■ You should regularly save your Web page to avoid losing your work.

FORMAT TEXT

You can make your Web page look more attractive by changing the design of the text.

You can increase or decrease the size of text on your Web page.

CHANGE THE FONT

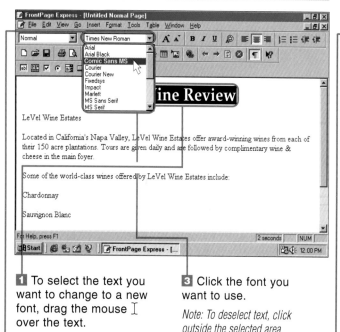

1 To select the text you want to change to a new font, drag the mouse I over the text.

2 Click this area to display a list of the available fonts.

3 Click the font you want to use.

Note: To deselect text, click outside the selected area.

CHANGE THE TEXT SIZE

1 To select the text you want to change to a new size, drag the mouse I over the text.

2 Click the size option you want to use.

A' Increase the text size.

A' Decrease the text size.

You can bold, italicize or underline text to emphasize information on your Web page.

You can change the color of text on your Web page.

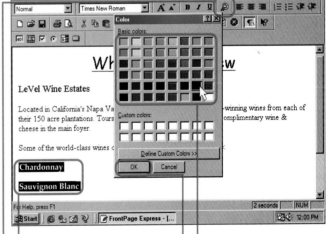

■ **BOLD, ITALICIZE OR UNDERLINE TEXT** ■

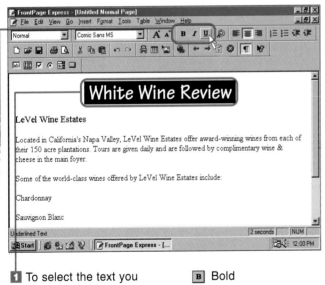

1 To select the text you want to change to a new style, drag the mouse I over the text.

2 Click the style you want to use.

B Bold

I Italic

U Underline

■ **COLOR TEXT** ■

1 To select the text you want to add color to, drag the mouse I over the text.

2 Click ⟠ to display the Color dialog box.

3 Click the color you want to use.

4 Click **OK**.

CONTINUED ➤

FORMAT TEXT

You can enhance the appearance of your Web page by aligning text in different ways.

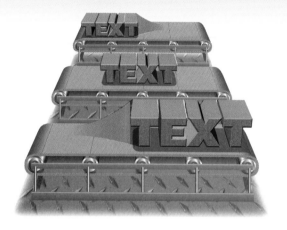

You can use the Indent feature to set off paragraphs on your Web page.

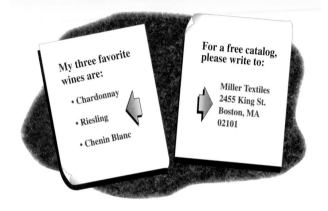

CHANGE TEXT ALIGNMENT

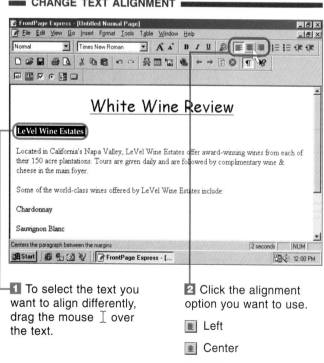

1 To select the text you want to align differently, drag the mouse I over the text.

2 Click the alignment option you want to use.

≣ Left

≣ Center

≣ Right

INDENT TEXT

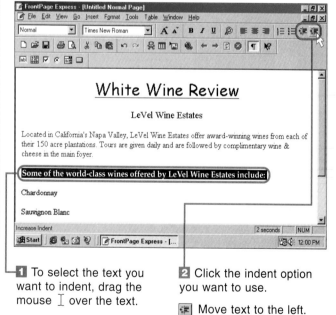

1 To select the text you want to indent, drag the mouse I over the text.

2 Click the indent option you want to use.

⧉ Move text to the left.

⧉ Move text to the right.

You can separate items
in a list by beginning
each item with a
number or bullet.

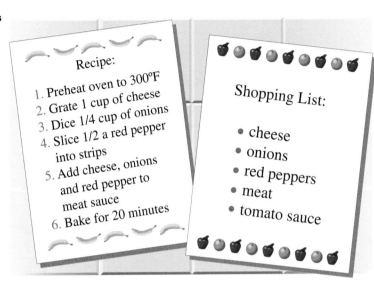

Numbers are useful
for items in a specific
order, such as a set
of instructions. Bullets
are useful for items
in no particular order,
such as a checklist.

■ CREATE A LIST

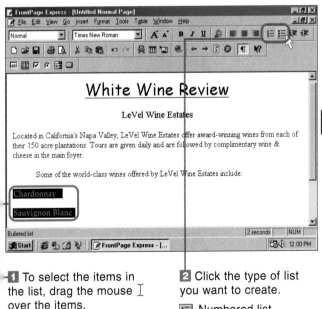

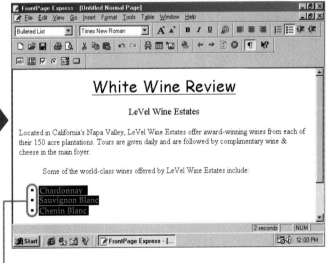

1 To select the items in
the list, drag the mouse I
over the items.

2 Click the type of list
you want to create.

▤ Numbered list

▤ Bulleted list

■ A number or bullet (•)
appears in front of each
item in the list.

*Note: To remove the numbers
or bullets from a list, repeat
steps 1 and 2.*

INSERT AN IMAGE

You can add images to your Web page to make the page more interesting and attractive.

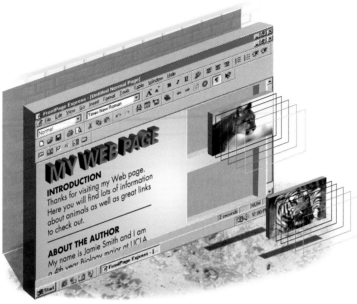

When adding images to your Web page, try to use images with the .gif or .jpg extension, since these are the most common types of images on the Web.

Before adding images to your Web page, place the images you want to use in the folder where your Web page is stored.

■ INSERT AN IMAGE ■

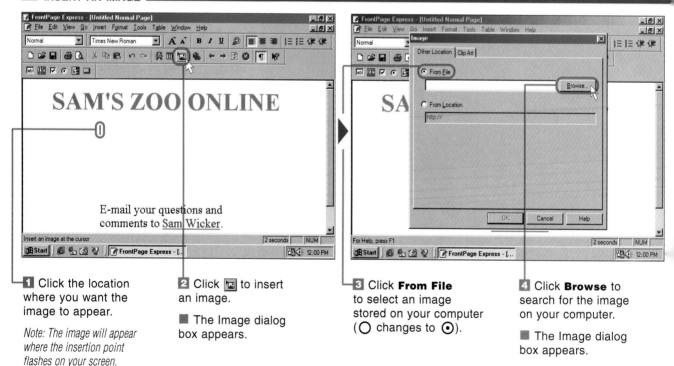

1 Click the location where you want the image to appear.

Note: The image will appear where the insertion point flashes on your screen.

2 Click ▣ to insert an image.

■ The Image dialog box appears.

3 Click **From File** to select an image stored on your computer (○ changes to ⊙).

4 Click **Browse** to search for the image on your computer.

■ The Image dialog box appears.

Where can I get images to use in my Web pages?

Many pages on the Web offer images you can use for free or you can buy a collection of ready-made images, called clip art, at most computer stores. You can also use a scanner to scan images into your computer or use a drawing program to create your own images. Make sure you have permission to use any images you do not create yourself.

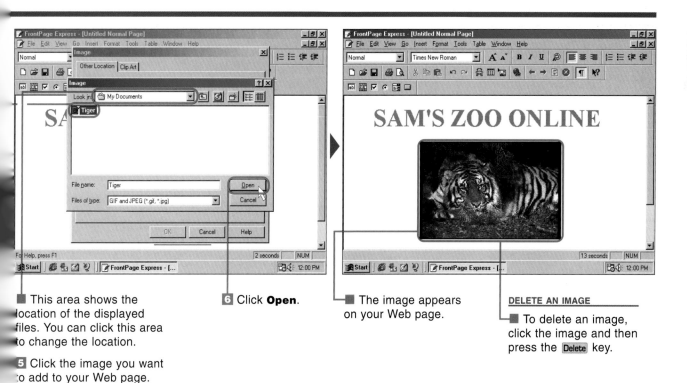

■ This area shows the location of the displayed files. You can click this area to change the location.

5 Click the image you want to add to your Web page.

6 Click **Open**.

■ The image appears on your Web page.

DELETE AN IMAGE

■ To delete an image, click the image and then press the Delete key.

ADD A BACKGROUND IMAGE

You can have a small image repeat to fill an entire Web page. This can add an interesting background texture to your page.

You can get background images at the following Web sites:

www.ecnet.net/
users/gas52r0/Jay/
backgrounds/back.htm

www.ender-design.com/
rg/backidx.html

■■■ ADD A BACKGROUND IMAGE ■■■

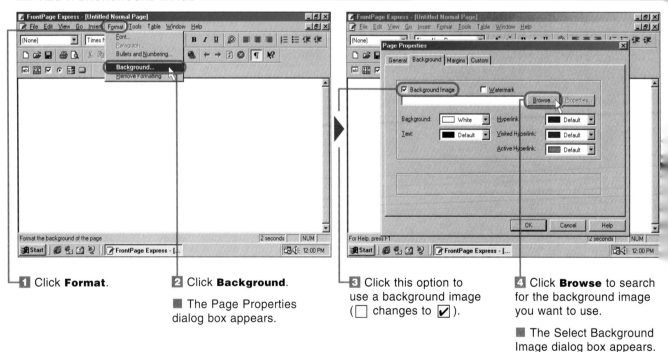

1 Click **Format**.

2 Click **Background**.

■ The Page Properties dialog box appears.

3 Click this option to use a background image (☐ changes to ✔).

4 Click **Browse** to search for the background image you want to use.

■ The Select Background Image dialog box appears.

What type of background image should I choose?

Choose an image that creates an interesting background design without overwhelming your Web page. Also make sure the image will not affect the readability of your Web page. To make the page easier to read, you may need to change the text color. See page 271 to change the color of text on a Web page.

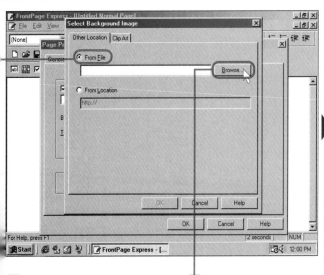

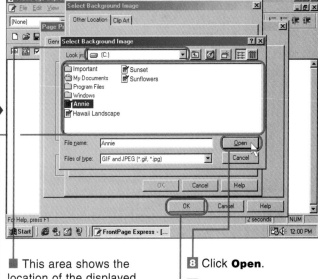

5 Click **From File** to select a background image stored on your computer (○ changes to ⊙).

6 Click **Browse** to search for the image on your computer.

■ The Select Background Image dialog box appears.

■ This area shows the location of the displayed files. You can click this area to change the location.

7 Click the image you want to use as the background image.

8 Click **Open**.

9 Click **OK** in the Page Properties dialog box.

■ The background image appears on your Web page.

CREATE A LINK

You can create a link to connect a word, phrase or image in your Web page to another Web page. When you select the text or image, the other Web page appears.

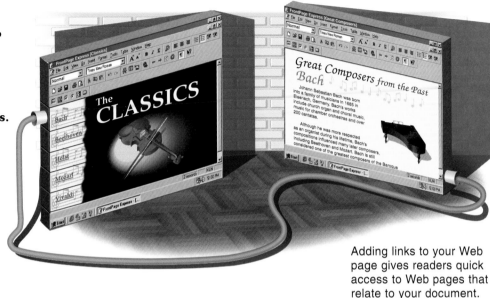

Adding links to your Web page gives readers quick access to Web pages that relate to your document.

CREATE A LINK

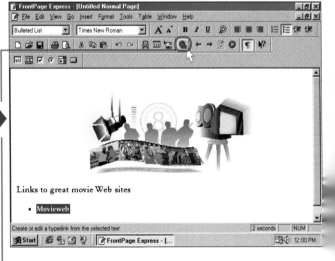

1 To select the text you want to link to another Web page, drag the mouse I over the text.

■ To select the image you want to link to another Web page, click the image.

2 Click 🔗 to create a link.

■ The Create Hyperlink dialog box appears.

How can I quickly create a link in my Web page?

When you type a Web page address or e-mail address, FrontPage Express automatically converts the address to a link for you.

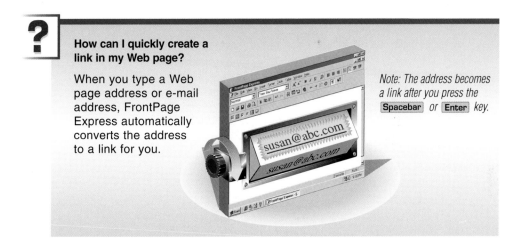

Note: The address becomes a link after you press the `Spacebar` *or* `Enter` *key.*

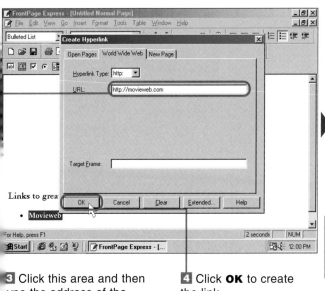

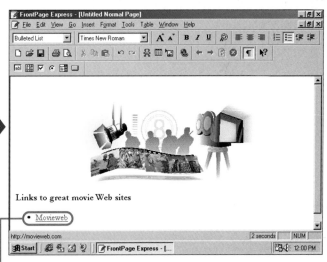

3 Click this area and then type the address of the Web page you want to link the text or image to.

4 Click **OK** to create the link.

■ FrontPage Express creates the link. Text links appear underlined and in color.

Note: To deselect text, click outside the selected area.

■ When you click the text or image in a Web browser, the Web page connected to the link will appear.

PUBLISH WEB PAGES

When you finish creating your Web page, you can transfer the page to a Web server. Once the Web page is stored on the server, your page will be available to everyone on the Web.

PUBLISH WEB PAGES

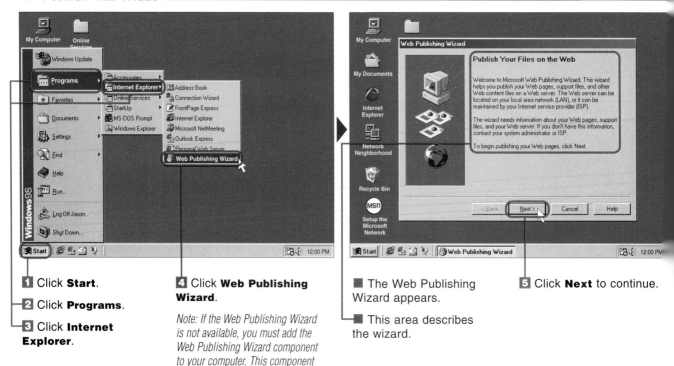

1 Click **Start**.

2 Click **Programs**.

3 Click **Internet Explorer**.

4 Click **Web Publishing Wizard**.

Note: If the Web Publishing Wizard is not available, you must add the Web Publishing Wizard component to your computer. This component is found in the Internet Tools category. To add a Windows component, see page 178.

■ The Web Publishing Wizard appears.

■ This area describes the wizard.

5 Click **Next** to continue.

Where can I publish my Web page?

The company that gives you
access to the Internet usually
offers space on its Web server
where you can publish your
Web page. There are also places
on the Internet that will publish
your Web page for free, such as
GeoCities (www.geocities.com).

You can also publish your Web
page on a corporate intranet. An
intranet is a small version of the
Internet within a company or
organization. Ask your system
administrator for details.

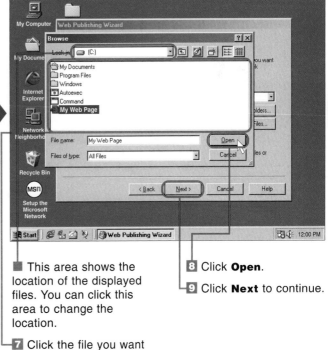

■ The wizard asks you
to enter the name of the
file you want to publish.

6 Click **Browse Files**
to locate the file on your
computer that you want
to publish.

■ The Browse dialog
box appears.

■ This area shows the
location of the displayed
files. You can click this
area to change the
location.

7 Click the file you want
to publish.

8 Click **Open**.

9 Click **Next** to continue.

CONTINUED ▶

PUBLISH WEB PAGES

You need to enter information about your Web server to publish your Web page. If you do not have this information, ask your Internet service provider or system administrator.

You must know the following information to publish your Web page:

• Address you use to access your personal Web pages

• User name

• Password

PUBLISH WEB PAGES (CONTINUED)

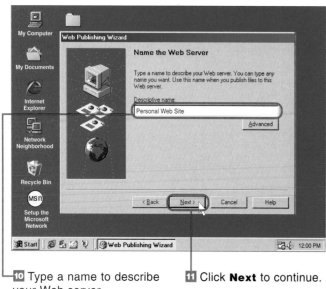

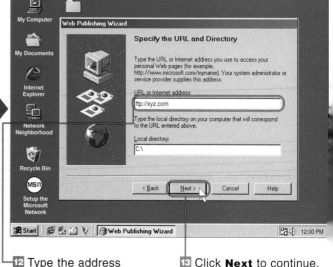

10 Type a name to describe your Web server.

Note: If you have published Web pages before, the wizard fills in the name of the Web server for you.

11 Click **Next** to continue.

12 Type the address you use to access your personal Web pages.

Note: If you have published Web pages before, this dialog box does not appear.

13 Click **Next** to continue.

?

If my Web page contains images, do I also need to publish the images?

If your Web page contains images or a background image, you also need to publish these files. If you do not publish the image files, an icon appears where the images should appear.

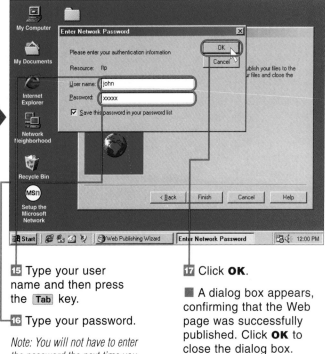

■ The wizard is ready to publish your Web page.

14 Click **Finish** to publish the Web page.

15 Type your user name and then press the **Tab** key.

16 Type your password.

Note: You will not have to enter the password the next time you publish Web pages.

17 Click **OK**.

■ A dialog box appears, confirming that the Web page was successfully published. Click **OK** to close the dialog box.

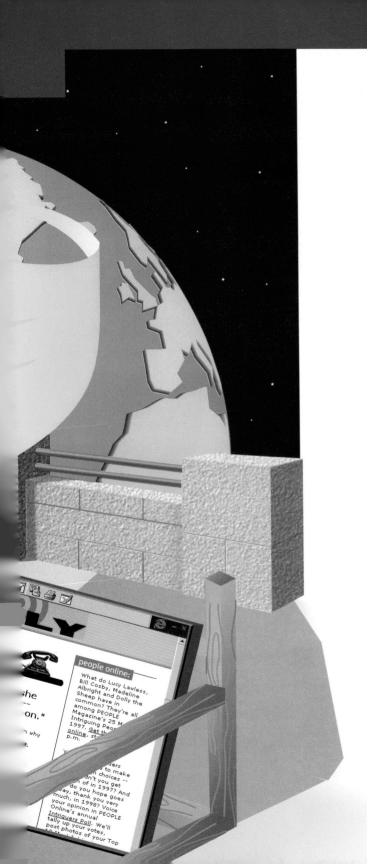

CHAPTER 14

Work With Channels

Read this chapter and learn how you can use channels to deliver Web content directly to your desktop.

ADD A CHANNEL

A channel is a Web site that automatically delivers information from the Internet to your computer. You can add channels of interest to you.

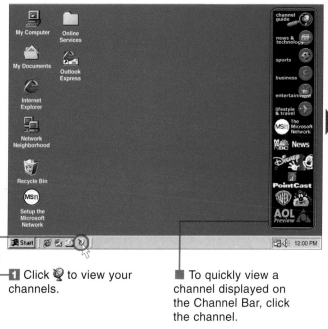

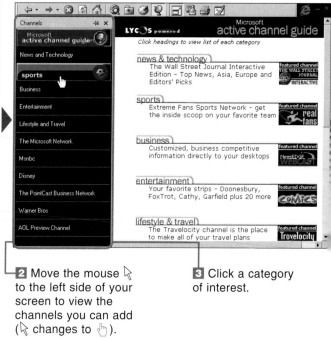

1 Click 🌐 to view your channels.

■ To quickly view a channel displayed on the Channel Bar, click the channel.

Note: If the Channel Bar is not on your desktop, see page 292 to display the Channel Bar.

2 Move the mouse ⬁ to the left side of your screen to view the channels you can add (⬁ changes to 👆).

3 Click a category of interest.

286

?

Why does the Channel Screen Saver dialog box appear?

Some channels include a screen saver you can use. The screen saver will appear on your screen when you do not use your computer for a period of time. For more information on screen savers, see page 114.

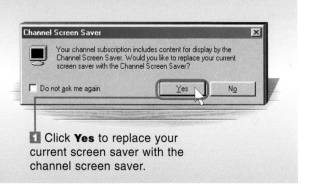

1 Click **Yes** to replace your current screen saver with the channel screen saver.

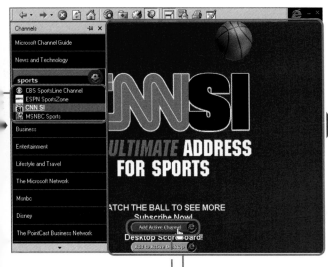

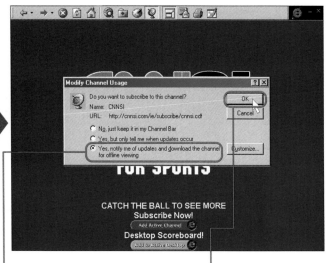

■ A list of channels in the category appears.

4 Click a channel of interest.

■ The channel appears.

5 Click **Add Active Channel** or the button that allows you to add the channel.

■ A dialog box appears.

6 Click this option to be notified of updates and to transfer the channel to your computer (○ changes to ⊙).

7 Click **OK** to add the channel.

ADD AN ACTIVE DESKTOP ITEM

You can add active content from the Web to your desktop. Active content is information that changes on your screen, such as a stock ticker or a weather map.

ADD AN ACTIVE DESKTOP ITEM

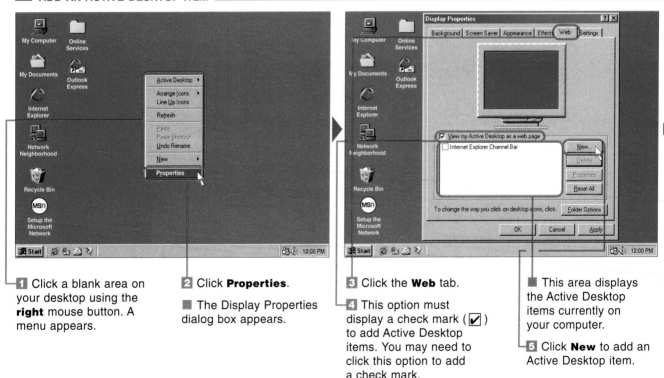

1 Click a blank area on your desktop using the **right** mouse button. A menu appears.

2 Click **Properties**.

■ The Display Properties dialog box appears.

3 Click the **Web** tab.

4 This option must display a check mark (☑) to add Active Desktop items. You may need to click this option to add a check mark.

■ This area displays the Active Desktop items currently on your computer.

5 Click **New** to add an Active Desktop item.

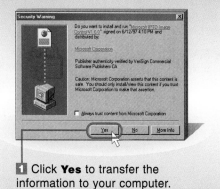

Why does the Security Warning dialog box appear?

The Security Warning dialog box may appear when you visit the Active Desktop Gallery. Microsoft may need to transfer information to your computer.

■1 Click **Yes** to transfer the information to your computer.

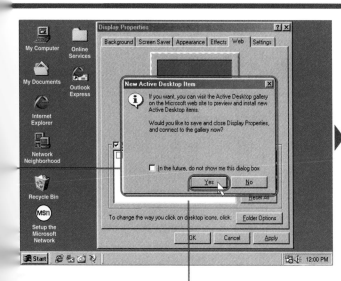

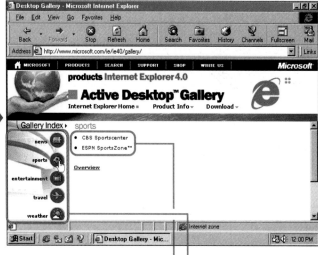

■ A dialog box appears, asking if you want to visit the gallery where you can see a list of Active Desktop items.

■6 Click **Yes** to visit the gallery.

Note: If you are not connected to the Internet, a dialog box may appear that allows you to connect.

■ The Internet Explorer Web browser opens and the Active Desktop Gallery appears.

Note: To maximize the window to fill your screen, click ▣ in the top right corner of the window.

■7 Click a category to display Active Desktop items of interest.

■ This area displays the Active Desktop items in the category you selected.

CONTINUED

ADD AN ACTIVE DESKTOP ITEM

The Active Desktop Gallery offers various items you can add to your desktop. The items are organized into categories such as news, sports, entertainment and weather.

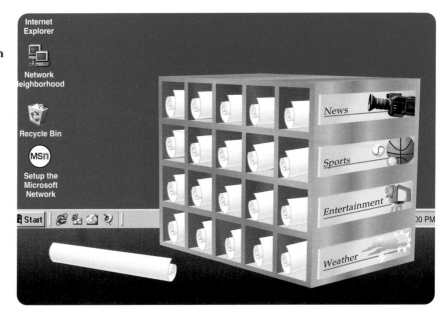

■ **ADD AN ACTIVE DESKTOP ITEM** (CONTINUED) ■

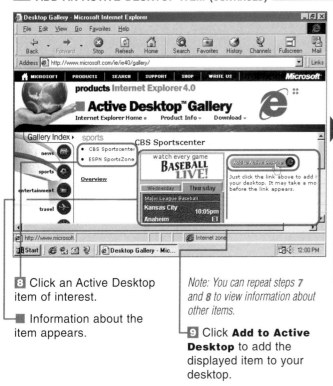

8 Click an Active Desktop item of interest.

■ Information about the item appears.

Note: You can repeat steps 7 and 8 to view information about other items.

9 Click **Add to Active Desktop** to add the displayed item to your desktop.

■ The Security Alert dialog box appears.

10 Click **Yes** to add the item to your desktop.

Why does the Active Desktop Gallery look different on my computer?

Companies, organizations and individuals constantly make changes to their Web pages to update information and improve their Web sites. The Web page shown on your screen may look different from the Web page shown in this book.

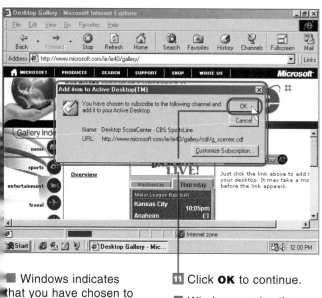

■ Windows indicates that you have chosen to subscribe to the channel and add it to your desktop.

11 Click **OK** to continue.

■ Windows copies the necessary information to your computer.

12 Click 📄 to minimize all open windows so you can clearly view your desktop.

■ The Active Desktop item appears on your screen.

Note: To move or remove the item, see page 292.

WORK WITH ACTIVE DESKTOP ITEMS

You can temporarily remove an Active Desktop item you no longer want to appear on your desktop. You can redisplay the item at any time.

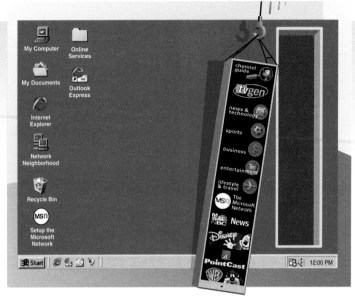

The Internet Explorer Channel Bar is an Active Desktop item that appears when you first start Windows. You can remove or display the Channel Bar as you would any other Active Desktop item.

REMOVE OR DISPLAY AN ITEM

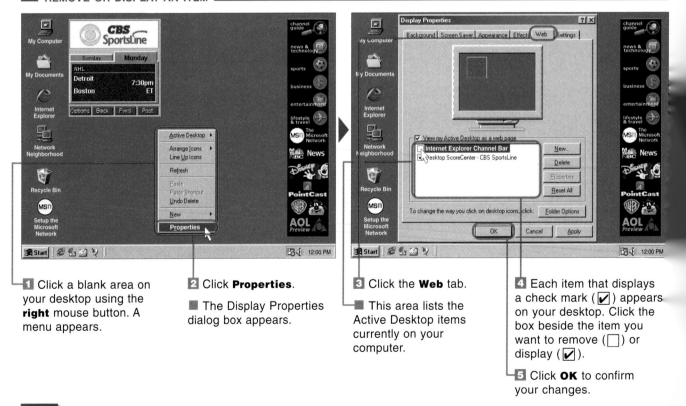

1 Click a blank area on your desktop using the **right** mouse button. A menu appears.

2 Click **Properties**.

■ The Display Properties dialog box appears.

3 Click the **Web** tab.

■ This area lists the Active Desktop items currently on your computer.

4 Each item that displays a check mark (✔) appears on your desktop. Click the box beside the item you want to remove (☐) or display (✔).

5 Click **OK** to confirm your changes.

You can move an Active Desktop item to a new location on your desktop.

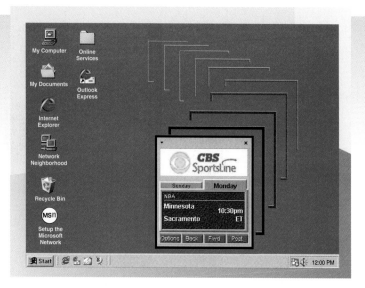

MOVE AN ITEM

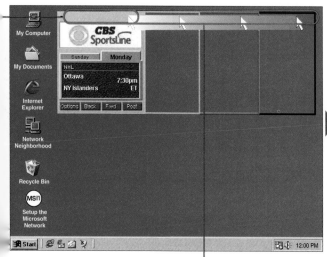

1 Position the mouse ▷ over the top edge of the item. A gray bar appears.

2 Drag the item to a new location on your desktop.

■ The item appears in the new location.

INDEX

INDEX

documents. *See also* files
- create, 4, 30-31
- open, 38-39
- print, 37
- save, 36
- text
  - align, 43
  - bold, 42
  - copy, 35
  - delete, 33
  - edit, 32-33
  - enter, 31
  - font size, change, 41
  - font type, change, 40
  - insert, 32
  - italic, 42
  - move, 34-35
  - underline, 42
  - undo changes, 33
domain names in e-mail addresses, 231
double-click
- speed, change, 126
- using mouse, 7
double-density floppy disks, 155
downloaded program files, delete, 168-169
Drafts folder, 235
drag and drop, using mouse, 7
draw
- lines in Paint, 50-51
- shapes in Paint, 48-49
drivers, printer, 187
drives, view contents, 62-63, 70-73

E

edit text, 32-33
e-mail
- address book
  - add names, 238-239
  - select names from, 240-241
- addresses
  - famous, 233
  - overview, 231
  - use as links, 279
- convenience of, 230
- cost of, 230
- exchange using Windows, 5
- messages
  - add signature, 248-249
  - attach files to, 242-243
  - compose, 236-237
  - delete, 247
  - forward, 246
  - get new, 235
  - read, 234-235
  - reply to, 244-245
  - view attached files, 243
- overview, 230-231
electronic mail. *See* e-mail
emoticons, in e-mail messages, 231
empty Recycle Bin, 92-93
enlarge. *See* maximize windows
equipment, share, using networks, 194
erase
- floppy disks, 154-157
- pictures in Paint, 54
ergonomic keyboards, 191
errors on disks, detect and repair, 160-163
Excite, Web search tool, 226
exit. *See also* close
- CD Player, 144
- Paint, 47
- Windows 98, 23
- WordPad, 31

F

FAQ (Frequently Asked Questions), 259
Favorites, Web pages
- add, 222-223
- view, 223
files. *See also* documents
- add to Start menu, 137
- attach to e-mail messages, 242-243
- cancel printing, 97
- close, 76
- copy, 85
  - to floppy disks, 86-87
- delete, 88-89
  - from Recycle Bin, 168-169
- deselect, 79
- display information for, 64-65
- downloaded program, delete, 168-169
- find, 98-101
- move, 84-85
- names, Web pages, 269
- open, 76, 77
- print, 94-95
- printing, cancel, 97
- rename, 80-81
- restore deleted, 90-91
- select, 78-79
- share, using networks, 194
- sharing
  - turn off, 197
  - turn on, 195-197
- shortcuts, add to desktop, 102-103
- sort, 66-67

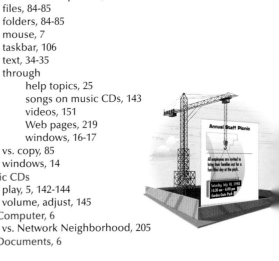

INDEX

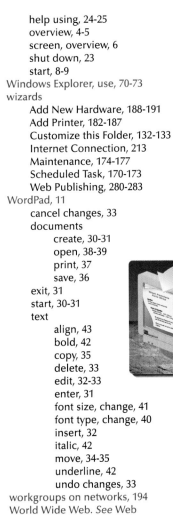

Y